An Analysis of

Ha-Joon Chang's

Kicking Away
the Ladder
Development Strategy in
Historical Perspective

Sulaiman Hakemy

Published by Macat International Ltd
24:13 Coda Centre, 189 Munster Road, London SW6 6AW.

Distributed exclusively by Routledge
2 Park Square, Milton Park, Abingdon, Oxon OX14 4RN
711 Third Avenue, New York, NY 10017, USA

Routledge is an imprint of the Taylor & Francis Group, an informa business

www.macat.com
info@macat.com

Cataloguing in Publication Data
A catalogue record for this book is available from the British Library.
Library of Congress Cataloguing-in-Publication Data is available upon request.
Cover illustration: Gérard Goffaux

ISBN 978-1-912302-20-8 (hardback)
ISBN 978-1-912128-93-8 (paperback)
ISBN 978-1-912281-08-4 (e-book)

Notice
The information in this book is designed to orientate readers of the work under analysis,
to elucidate and contextualise its key ideas and themes, and to aid in the development
of critical thinking skills. It is not meant to be used, nor should it be used, as a
substitute for original thinking or in place of original writing or research. References and
notes are provided for informational purposes and their presence does not constitute
endorsement of the information or opinions therein. This book is presented solely for
educational purposes. It is sold on the understanding that the publisher is not engaged
to provide any scholarly advice. The publisher has made every effort to ensure that
this book is accurate and up-to-date, but makes no warranties or representations with
regard to the completeness or reliability of the information it contains. The information
and the opinions provided herein are not guaranteed or warranted to produce particular
results and may not be suitable for students of every ability. The publisher shall not be
liable for any loss, damage or disruption arising from any errors or omissions, or from
the use of this book, including, but not limited to, special, incidental, consequential or
other damages caused, or alleged to have been caused, directly or indirectly, by the
information contained within.

CONTENTS

WAYS IN TO THE TEXT

Who Is Ha-Joon Chang? 9

What Does *Kicking Away the Ladder* Say? 11

Why Does *Kicking Away the Ladder* Matter? 12

SECTION 1: INFLUENCES

Module 1: The Author and the Historical Context 16

Module 2: Academic Context 20

Module 3: The Problem 25

Module 4: The Author's Contribution 29

SECTION 2: IDEAS

Module 5: Main Ideas 34

Module 6: Secondary Ideas 39

Module 7: Achievement 44

Module 8: Place in the Author's Work 47

SECTION 3: IMPACT

Module 9: The First Responses 52

Module 10: The Evolving Debate 56

Module 11: Impact and Influence Today 60

Module 12: Where Next? 64

Glossary of Terms 69

People Mentioned in the Text 78

Works Cited 84

THE MACAT LIBRARY

The Macat Library is a series of unique academic explorations of seminal works in the humanities and social sciences – books and papers that have had a significant and widely recognised impact on their disciplines. It has been created to serve as much more than just a summary of what lies between the covers of a great book. It illuminates and explores the influences on, ideas of, and impact of that book. Our goal is to offer a learning resource that encourages critical thinking and fosters a better, deeper understanding of important ideas.

Each publication is divided into three Sections: Influences, Ideas, and Impact. Each Section has four Modules. These explore every important facet of the work, and the responses to it.

This Section-Module structure makes a Macat Library book easy to use, but it has another important feature. Because each Macat book is written to the same format, it is possible (and encouraged!) to cross-reference multiple Macat books along the same lines of inquiry or research. This allows the reader to open up interesting interdisciplinary pathways.

To further aid your reading, lists of glossary terms and people mentioned are included at the end of this book (these are indicated by an asterisk [*] throughout) – as well as a list of works cited.

Macat has worked with the University of Cambridge to identify the elements of critical thinking and understand the ways in which six different skills combine to enable effective thinking.
Three allow us to fully understand a problem; three more give us the tools to solve it. Together, these six skills make up the **PACIER** model of critical thinking. They are:

ANALYSIS – understanding how an argument is built
EVALUATION – exploring the strengths and weaknesses of an argument
INTERPRETATION – understanding issues of meaning

CREATIVE THINKING – coming up with new ideas and fresh connections
PROBLEM-SOLVING – producing strong solutions
REASONING – creating strong arguments

To find out more, visit **WWW.MACAT.COM.**

CRITICAL THINKING AND *KICKING AWAY THE LADDER*

Primary critical thinking skill: CREATIVE THINKING
Secondary critical thinking skill: REASONING

South Korean economist Ha-Joon Chang used his 2003 work *Kicking Away The Ladder* to challenge the central orthodoxies of development economics, using his creative thinking skills to shine new light on an old topic.

Creative thinkers are often distinguished by their willingness to challenge received ideas, and this is a central aspect of Chang's work on development. Before Chang, the received wisdom was that developing countries needed the same kinds of economic policies and institutions as developed countries in order to enjoy the same prosperity. But, as Chang pointed out, the historical evidence showed that First World economic success was, in fact, due to exactly the kinds of state intervention that modern development orthodoxy shuns. Western affluence is the product of precisely the kinds of state control – of protectionism and the setting of price tariffs – that developed countries have since denied the developing world in the name of economic freedom and 'best practice.'

By insisting that Third World nations should adopt these economic policies themselves, argued Chang, the West is actually stifling Third World economic prospects – kicking away the ladder. His carefully reasoned argument for a novel point of view was closely based on the critical thinking skill of producing novel explanations for existing evidence, and led many to question development orthodoxies – sparking a rethink of modern development strategies for less-developed countries.

ABOUT THE AUTHOR OF THE ORIGINAL WORK

Ha-Joon Chang was born in Seoul, South Korea, in 1963—a critical time in the country's history. South Korea's military government embarked on a period of rigidly directed economic expansion that within 20 years transformed one of the world's poorest countries into one of the richest. As a graduate student at the University of Cambridge University, Chang developed an economic theory suggesting that poor countries could thrive, not by adopting the free-market beliefs widely promoted in the West, but by implementing state-directed economic policies of the sort that had so spectacularly succeeded in South Korea. Chang remains perhaps the best-known champion of state-led economic initiatives, and in 2014, he was named one of the top 10 thinkers in the world by Prospect magazine.

ABOUT THE AUTHOR OF THE ANALYSIS

Sulaiman Hakemy holds an MSc in economic history and development from the London School of Economics. A writer and journalist, he has reported on industry, politics, and culture for various publications. His background is in the development aid and urban planning sectors, specialising in conflict and fragile states. He is based in Istanbul and Toronto, and speaks English, French, Spanish, Arabic, Persian, and some Urdu.

ABOUT MACAT

GREAT WORKS FOR CRITICAL THINKING

Macat is focused on making the ideas of the world's great thinkers accessible and comprehensible to everybody, everywhere, in ways that promote the development of enhanced critical thinking skills.

It works with leading academics from the world's top universities to produce new analyses that focus on the ideas and the impact of the most influential works ever written across a wide variety of academic disciplines. Each of the works that sit at the heart of its growing library is an enduring example of great thinking. But by setting them in context – and looking at the influences that shaped their authors, as well as the responses they provoked – Macat encourages readers to look at these classics and game-changers with fresh eyes. Readers learn to think, engage and challenge their ideas, rather than simply accepting them.

"Macat offers an amazing first-of-its-kind tool for interdisciplinary learning and research. Its focus on works that transformed their disciplines and its rigorous approach, drawing on the world's leading experts and educational institutions, opens up a world-class education to anyone."

Andreas Schleicher
Director for Education and Skills, Organisation for Economic Co-operation and Development

'Macat is taking on some of the major challenges in university education … They have drawn together a strong team of active academics who are producing teaching materials that are novel in the breadth of their approach.'

Prof Lord Broers,
former Vice-Chancellor of the University of Cambridge

'The Macat vision is exceptionally exciting. It focuses upon new modes of learning which analyse and explain seminal texts which have profoundly influenced world thinking and so social and economic development. It promotes the kind of critical thinking which is essential for any society and economy. This is the learning of the future.'

Rt Hon Charles Clarke, former UK Secretary of State for Education

'The Macat analyses provide immediate access to the critical conversation surrounding the books that have shaped their respective discipline, which will make them an invaluable resource to all of those, students and teachers, working in the field.'

Professor William Tronzo, University of California at San Diego

WAYS IN TO THE TEXT

KEY POINTS

- Ha-Joon Chang is a South Korean economist specializing in international development: the process by which a nation advances its prosperity, infrastructure, and living standards; he is a renowned critic of neoliberalism* (the belief that economic growth is best secured by limiting government economic intervention).

- *Kicking Away the Ladder* (2003) critically examines the economic histories* of the richest countries in the world today. It argues that their success was the result of precisely those policies they now claim are inappropriate for development in poor countries.

- An influential work in development literature, *Kicking Away the Ladder* was the first book to cite a wide range of examples of Western economic histories in order to challenge effectively neoliberal development theory.

Who Is Ha-Joon Chang?

Born in South Korea in 1963, Ha-Joon Chang, the author of *Kicking Away the Ladder: Development Strategy in Historical Perspective* (2003), is a development economist at Cambridge University in England. He grew up in Korea during its transformation from an impoverished developing nation into one of the richest in the world. He completed graduate studies in Cambridge under the Marxist* economist Robert Rowthorn;* "Marxist" refers to the social and political analysis of the nineteenth-century political philosopher Karl Marx, who understood history to be driven, primarily, by conflict between social classes. Rowthorn's ideas, along with those of other economists of the "heterodox school,"* who dispute mainstream economic teaching, were a major influence on Chang.

The economic success of South Korea was the result of state intervention in the economy, primarily in the form of subsidies for key industries and protection from foreign competition. In spite of this experience, the dominant economic belief in rich nations, known to economists as now-developed countries* or NDCs, was that states should not interfere with the free market* (trade without regulation or restriction). This neoliberalism was in turn imposed on poor "Third World"* countries, what economists call less-developed countries (LDCs),* by policymakers from developed "First World"* nations through economic aid programs they financed. Yet such neoliberal reforms failed to shield many less-developed countries from economic crises in the 1990s and early 2000s; in some cases, they even exacerbated them.

Chang found himself questioning the theory and history of neoliberalism. The result was the trenchant criticism of neoliberalism for which Chang is best known today.

Published in 2003, *Kicking Away the Ladder* was Chang's first book aimed at nonspecialist readers. Its success won him a high public profile as a critic of free-market fundamentalism and development policy. Chang continues to teach at Cambridge and has also worked as a consultant for various nongovernmental* and international organizations. In 2014, he was named one of the top 10 thinkers in the world by *Prospect* magazine.[1]

What Does *Kicking Away the Ladder* Say?

In *Kicking Away the Ladder*, Chang argues that we should question what we have been taught about the history of economic development—specifically, what made today's developed nations economic successes. By implication, this means that modern development strategies for less-developed countries need to be rethought. Chang's contention is that rich countries today—essentially, the West—developed successfully because of state interventions in markets, such as protectionism* (taxes or regulations serving to penalize international trade).

This exactly contradicts the conventional wisdom that they became successful through neoliberal policies and institutions:* free trade, minimal government control over the economy, and the dominance of private enterprise. Chang goes further, arguing that today's rich countries are concealing the "secrets of their success" from poor countries in urging them to institute neoliberal reforms and to forgo protectionism.[2] In Chang's view this amounts to "kicking away the ladder" from developing countries.

The book addresses three ideas.

The first is Chang's argument that the economic history of the developed world should influence development strategies in the developing world today; in his introductory chapter, Chang explains that his book examines the economic histories of the United States, Great Britain, and several other Western countries, in order to assess what kind of development strategies worked for them.

He then discusses the role of interventionist policies in economic development, presenting historical evidence to show that Western countries developed largely thanks to protectionism and active state support for new industries—the opposite of what these nations forcefully recommend to developing countries today.

In the book's third section, Chang outlines several examples of what the developed world calls the "good institutions"* held to be essential for strong economic development. These include democracy,* a judiciary (legal system) independent of outside influence, property rights* (rules protecting the ownership of physical or intellectual property), corporate governance* (the administration of profit-making companies on the basis of certain rules), financial institutions, social welfare* (protections for the nation's most vulnerable), and labor institutions* (rules and practices that protect the rights and well-being of workers). Again, Chang turns to the history of the NDCs, showing that, in many cases, these rich nations achieved economic development without these institutions. He concludes that many "good institutions" are in fact a *product* of development, rather than a *prerequisite* for it.

Chang's discussion of the institution of intellectual property* rights (rights regarding inventions, concepts, and so on) is particularly interesting. He cites several examples of persistent violation of intellectual property laws in European history. He then argues that intellectual property protection is not only unnecessary for economic development but may even be stifling development. Chang goes on to make equally controversial arguments about the nature of corruption. Contradicting the recommendations of most governments and development agencies, *Kicking Away the Ladder* suggests that fighting corruption is not crucial to economic development.

Chang presents all of these ideas concisely and simply. Most of *Kicking Away the Ladder*'s content consists of diverse and exhaustive historical examples. Yet, while it is an economic history, the book intends to influence contemporary economic policy. It brings together a broad range of research by economic historians and uses it to build an argument against neoliberalism in development.

Why Does *Kicking Away the Ladder* Matter?

Ha-Joon Chang begins *Kicking Away the Ladder* with a "health warning," writing, "What this book is about to say will undoubtedly disturb many people, both intellectually and morally."[3] Because of the boldness of its ideas, *Kicking Away the Ladder* was the first of Ha-Joon Chang's books to receive significant public attention. It was awarded the 2003 Gunnar Myrdal Prize by the European Association for Evolutionary Political Economy. It was also a major factor in Chang's being awarded the 2005 Wassily Leontief prize from the Global Development and Environment Institute. *Kicking Away the Ladder*'s accolades and commercial success together gave Ha-Joon Chang the status of a public intellectual and one of the most respected figures in development economics. This is particularly impressive, given his contrarian approach to the discipline. *Kicking Away the Ladder*'s popularity has helped to place many of Chang's most radical arguments in the mainstream of discussions about the role of capitalism* (the economic system dominant in the West today, in which business is conducted for private profit) and free trade* (trade conducted without governmental regulation or restriction).

One of *Kicking Away the Ladder*'s most important contributions is its unique methodology—the method Chang employed to reach his conclusions. While the book did not create any new schools of theory, and was not based on original research, it was the first to gather historical studies of rich countries in such depth and to build a broader argument against neoliberalism as an instrument of development. Chang's major critics disagree with this methodology—but Chang has defended it; for him, narratives based on nations were necessary "because of the difficulty involved in clearly identifying the existence and the intensity of particular policies."[4] Since the publication of *Kicking Away the Ladder*, Chang has published several more books and articles that develop and reinforce its initial ideas.

Although it was published comparatively recently and draws mainly on preexisting scholarship, *Kicking Away the Ladder* has exerted a substantial influence in current research. Chang's ideas have become the most prominent in a strain of development economics scholarship critical of free-trade policies. Since the global financial crisis* of 2008 and the European debt crisis,* which began at much the same time, criticism of free trade and capitalism has continued to grow. This gives *Kicking Away the Ladder* considerable importance in the continuing debate about the global economy today.

NOTES

1   "World Thinkers 2014: The Results," *Prospect*, accessed January 12, 2016, http://www.prospectmagazine.co.uk/features/world-thinkers-2014-the-results.

2   Ha-Joon Chang, *Kicking Away the Ladder: Development Strategy in Historical Perspective* (London: Anthem Press, 2003), 2.

3   Chang, *Kicking Away the Ladder*, 12.

4   Chang, *Kicking Away the Ladder*, 10.

SECTION 1
INFLUENCES

MODULE 1
THE AUTHOR AND THE
HISTORICAL CONTEXT

KEY POINTS

- *Kicking Away the Ladder* challenges the conventional wisdom on how poor countries can raise themselves economically to achieve the prosperity, infrastructure, and living standards of rich countries — "development."*

- Ha-Joon Chang was born and raised in South Korea at a time when the country was experiencing one of the most rapid transformations in economic development and quality of life in modern history.

- Chang's mentors were frustrated with the ineffectiveness of the orthodox development policies* imposed on developing countries* by the West.

Why Read This Text?

Ha-Joon Chang's *Kicking Away the Ladder: Development Strategy in Historical Perspective* (2003) offers a radical critique of what the policymakers of international monetary bodies and wealthy nations assert as being the most reliable means of ensuring economic development in poor countries. In this way, it builds a compelling counterargument to the conventional wisdom about why some countries are rich and others are poor.

Since the end of World War II* in 1945, economists and those with influence in international organizations in the rich, industrial First World* have exerted significant pressure on poor, developing countries to adopt what are seen as "good policies" and "good institutions"* in order to escape poverty.* *Kicking Away the Ladder*

> **❝** I don't do maths. A lot of economists think I'm not an economist. **❞**
>
> Ha-Joon Chang, *Financial Times*

tackles these conventional solutions directly and demonstrates that for many poor countries these "good policies" and "good institutions" are ineffective at best—if not actually harmful.

The book forces students of politics, economics, and development studies (the study of the history and processes of national development) to question the conventional wisdom of the international policymaking establishment and to rethink ideas of justice and equality between countries. *Kicking Away the Ladder* is highly critical of two highly influential financial institutions, the International Monetary Fund* (IMF) and the World Bank,* both of which play a central role in global economic development. Over a decade after its publication, the issues raised by Chang in *Kicking Away the Ladder* remain vitally important.

Author's Life

Ha-Joon Chang is a development economist: a scholar of economic issues concerning the development of poor nations. He was born in Seoul, South Korea, in 1963. His father was a civil servant in the South Korean Ministry of Finance who had grown up in poverty under brutal Japanese colonial* rule, and the privations imposed on Korea by World War II and the Korean War* (1950–53).

After receiving his BA in economics from Seoul National University, in 1986 Chang became a graduate student in England in the Faculty of Economics and Politics at Cambridge University. He received his PhD in 1992 for his thesis "The Political Economy* of Industrial Policy*—Reflections on the Role of State Intervention." At Cambridge, Chang's teachers sparked his interest in heterodox economics*—approaches to the study of economics outside the mainstream. His PhD supervisor was Robert Rowthorn,* an economist influenced by the economic and social analysis of the nineteenth-century political philosopher Karl Marx,* for whom material circumstances such as class and wealth were the principal drivers of historical events. With Rowthorn, Chang developed his theory of industrial policy (the strategy of achieving development through industrialization) as a middle way between central planning* (in which the government decides how resources are to be allocated) and free-market* (unregulated, profit-driven) perspectives of economic governance. Chang's move into development economics was also influenced by the renowned development economists Ajit Singh,* Gabriel Palma,* and Peter Nolan.*

Chang has remained at Cambridge since receiving his doctorate. In addition to his work as a teacher at the university, Chang has worked as a consultant for numerous nongovernmental organizations* (NGOs) and international organizations, including various United Nations* agencies. He has published 12 books.

Author's Background

Chang's upbringing in a South Korea in the grip of a radical social and economic transformation in the 1960s and '70s significantly shaped him: "Korea, one of the poorest countries in the world, was the sorry country I was born into … Today, I am a citizen of one of the wealthier, if not wealthiest, countries in the world. During my lifetime, per capita income in Korea has grown something like 14 times, in purchasing power terms."[1] These changes were driven by the military dictatorship of General Park Chung-Hee,* whose policies mandated that "spending foreign exchange on anything not essential for industrial development was prohibited."[2] This included foreign travel— meaning that Chang had never left Korea before travelling to study at Cambridge in 1986.

When Chang began university in Seoul in 1982, South Korea had become a middle-income country thanks in large part to its ability to "reverse engineer"* and to copy advanced industrial products from the West. But the country still struggled to produce original products and to develop international patents, copyrights, and trademarks. The country's struggles in these areas sparked Chang's interest in intellectual property rights* (protections of the ownership of ideas and inventions) which would remain a central concern of his academic career.

In the wider world, the Washington Consensus*—a set of more or less universally accepted Western policies, easing the regulations and restrictions affecting private activity in the economy ("economic liberalization")*—was considered the standard doctrine in addressing the development needs of poor countries. Development economists like Chang and his mentors were increasingly frustrated with the fact that, throughout the 1990s and early 2000s, developing countries that had followed the prescriptions of the Washington Consensus (Mexico in 1995, much of Southeast Asia in 1997, Bulgaria and Romania the same year, Argentina in 2000–1) experienced financial crises and economic recession.* *Kicking Away the Ladder* is a product of this frustration and Chang's assertion that critics of the Washington Consensus had not collected enough evidence for their argument from the history of the developed countries* themselves.

NOTES

1   Ha-Joon Chang, *Bad Samaritans: The Myth of Free Trade and the Secret History of Capitalism* (New York: Bloomsbury Press, 2008), x.

2   Chang, *Bad Samaritans*, xiv.

MODULE 2
ACADEMIC CONTEXT

KEY POINTS

- *Kicking Away the Ladder* suggests that a study of the economic history of rich nations can be useful in deciding development* strategies for poor nations, allowing them to achieve similar levels of prosperity, comfort, and advanced infrastructure.

- While development economics*—the study of economics related to this process—has seen significant debate since the 1940s, by the end of the twentieth century neoliberalism,* with its emphasis on private control of the economy, had become the dominant orthodoxy of Western economic policymaking.

- Chang's criticisms of neoliberalism were reinforced by his academic mentors and his observations of its failures in the real world.

The Work in its Context

While the lack of mathematical analysis in his work has often led to Ha-Joon Chang being labeled as a political scientist* or sociologist* rather than as an economist, there can be no question that his *Kicking Away the Ladder* is preeminently a work of economics. There can be no question, either, that it directly challenges orthodox economic thinking on development economics (a field in which it is widely regarded as especially influential).

Development economics is the branch of economics concerned with how poor, developing countries* can increase their wealth and the quality of life of their citizens. But this is more than a matter of economics alone: wider questions of politics, sociology, and other

> **❝ 95% of economics is common sense deliberately made complicated. ❞**
> Ha-Joon Chang, lecture at the Royal Society of Arts

social sciences invariably have to be taken into consideration.

However, it remains true that in such developing countries "governments needed guidance from economists on how to make economic development happen differently—and, especially, faster—in the future."[1] As a book concerned with overturning assumptions about government-engineered economic transformation by looking at how today's developed nations transformed themselves, *Kicking Away the Ladder* addresses the concerns of development economics to ask what lessons can be learned about how and why the world's rich nations became rich.

Overview of the Field

Development economics emerged in the 1940s as a forward-looking field distinguished by its "exploration of the problem of government-engineered economic transformation."[2] In the first half of the twentieth century, the debate within development economics concerned whether development occurs in linear stages (A leading to B, leading to C, all finally leading to transformation), as argued by the economic historian* Walt Rostow,* or through structural change (a set of social policies deliberately pursued to achieve a desired economic transformation), as argued by the development economist William Arthur Lewis.*

Rostow maintained that governments can achieve growth by increasing their rates of savings* and investment.* Lewis, influenced by the Polish economist Paul Rosenstein-Rodan,* argued that the priority should be urbanization* and industrialization*—the transformations that arrive through moving from a rural and agricultural to an urban and industrial society and economy.

Governments must therefore harness "surplus labor" from the agricultural sector and, through training programs, give workers the skills to move into industrial work. Lewis's approach was the inspiration for the key 1951 United Nations* report, *Measures for the Economic Development of Under-Developed Countries.*[3]

In the 1970s, the "international dependency approach" gained prominence, especially in developing countries themselves. According to this approach, development fails either because of the harmful legacy of colonialism*—specifically the exploitation by European nations of lands and people in Africa, Asia, the Americas, and so on—or the flawed advice given by international financial institutions* (IFIs).

In the 1980s, development economics saw a reaction from economists of the neoclassical* school, who asserted that free-market principles could adequately address development needs and that the state should *minimize* its intervention. This way of thinking also came to be called "neoliberalism" by Chang and other development economists outside the United States.

In spite of the fact that it is rejected by a growing number of economists, the neoliberal approach continues to dominate Western policymaking circles today. Within development economics, the measurable failures of neoclassical development theory have ushered in a new approach, known as endogenous growth theory,* which contends that economic growth can best be achieved by investments in education and in what is known as human capital* development: in brief, the better educated a country's population, the greater its economic potential.

Academic Influences

As an economist arguing against prevailing economic orthodoxies, Chang has been influenced by a diverse range of economic views. He was initially educated in neoclassical economics,[4] the dominant school of economic thought in the latter half of the twentieth century. While Chang has recognized that neoclassical economics "can provide us with some very useful tools to analyze problems within a given structure," his personal view is that "it is not very good at understanding how the institutions, technologies, politics, and ideas that define that structure evolve over time."[5]

Chang's position on neoclassical economics was shaped by observations from his home country, South Korea, and by the teachings of his academic mentors. Cambridge University, where Chang studied, is renowned for its Keynesian* approach to economics and opposition to neoliberal doctrines. Based on the thought of the economist John Maynard Keynes,* Keynesian economists acknowledge the beneficial role of certain forms of government intervention into a nation's economy. One of Chang's greatest influences during this period was his PhD supervisor, the leading Marxist* economist Robert Rowthorn.*

Three academics in the fields of development economics and economic history were particularly influential in Chang's arguments in *Kicking Away the Ladder*. Erik Reinert,* a Norwegian economist known for his 2007 book *How Rich Countries Got Rich and Why Poor Countries Stay Poor*,[6] offered sources in economic history around which Chang's research is crafted. The development studies professor James Putzel's* ideas on the role of institutional development "provided the critical impetus to get [*Kicking Away the Ladder*] going."[7] Finally, the economic historian Charles Kindleberger* provided early reactions to Chang's thoughts, allowing Chang to develop a more robust defense of the book's key points.

NOTES

1   John Toye, "Changing Perspectives in Development Economics," in *Rethinking Development Economics*, ed. Ha-Joon Chang (London and New York: Anthem Press, 2003), 21.

2   Toye, "Changing Perspectives in Development Economics," 21.

3   Toye, "Changing Perspectives in Development Economics," 23.

4   "Economists Who Have Influenced Me," Ha-Joon Chang, accessed January 12, 2016, http://hajoonchang.net/economists-who-have-influenced-me/.

5   "Economists Who Have Influenced Me."

6   Erik S. Reinert, *How Rich Countries Got Rich … and Why Poor Countries Stay Poor* (London: Constable, 2007).

7   Ha-Joon Chang, *Kicking Away the Ladder: Development Strategy in Historical Perspective* (London: Anthem Press, 2003), vi.

MODULE 3
THE PROBLEM

KEY POINTS

- The core question in *Kicking Away the Ladder* is whether rich countries today are inadvertently rigging the international economic system against poor countries by preventing them from enacting effective development* strategies.

- The twentieth century saw neoliberalism* (roughly, the notion that the unhindered pursuit of private profit was the most effective route to economic prosperity) become the dominant ideology of economic development among global policymakers.

- At the time of *Kicking Away the Ladder*'s publication, discontent with the apparent ineffectiveness of neoliberal economics was growing.

Core Question

In *Kicking Away the Ladder: Development Strategy in Historical Perspective*, Ha-Joon Chang wants to understand whether today's rich countries, which he calls now-developed countries* (NDCs), had followed the prescriptions of the Washington Consensus* in the course of their own economic development. In the 1970s and 1980s, international financial institutions* (IFIs) and the government of the United States developed a set of policy and institutional reforms that they believed were fundamental prerequisites for all developing countries*—or less-developed countries* (LDCs)—to achieve economic growth.* "The Washington Consensus" is how this set of prescriptions, which took a neoliberal view of globalization* arguing in favor of free markets and against state intervention, became known.

> ❝ It is a very common device that whenever anyone has attained the summit of greatness, he kicks away the ladder by which he has climbed up, in order to deprive others of the means of climbing up after him. ❞
>
> Friedrich List, *The National System of Political Economy*

Chang has two reasons for asking the question. The first is the apparent ineffectiveness of Washington Consensus policies in pulling developing countries out of poverty and underdevelopment. The second is the clear success of alternative strategies that many developing countries have used. Chang declares at the start of the book that "the short answer to this question is that the developed countries* did not get where they are now through the policies and institutions that they recommend to developing countries today."[1] *Kicking Away the Ladder* explores the evidence supporting this conclusion, and in doing so suggests that NDCs are obstructing, or even exploiting, the economies of LDCs by continuing to preach supposed practices for success that they themselves had never adopted.

The Participants

Development economics* as a field of study evolved in an attempt to explain how any country develops and grows economically. In the mid-twentieth century, the economists Walt Rostow,*[2] Simon Kuznets,*[3] and William Arthur Lewis*[4] all formulated theories of the stages of economic development based on the history of industrialization* in successful developed countries ("industrialization" here signifying the move from an economy based on agriculture to one based on industry). The underlying question of whether or not it is best for a nation's economy if its government allows it to operate unhindered, without regulation or intervention, was investigated by thinkers such as Adam Smith,*[5] Friedrich List,*[6] and Alexander

Hamilton[*7] in the eighteenth and nineteenth centuries.

Toward the end of the twentieth century, the debate was actively taken up in political circles and by the international institutions of an increasingly globalized world. Conservative politicians such the American president Ronald Reagan* and the British prime minister Margaret Thatcher,* along with World Bank* chief economist Anne Kreuger,* were strong advocates of neoliberalism. Indeed, the World Bank, with the International Monetary Fund* (IMF), promoted neoliberal economic practices through structural adjustment programs:* offering loans to countries experiencing economic crises on condition that those countries institute neoliberal economic reforms to their institutions* and economic policies.*

The Contemporary Debate

At the time of *Kicking Away the Ladder*'s publication, the intellectual debate was divided between neoliberals—primarily policymakers, bureaucrats from international financial institutions (IFIs), and the economists who supported their work—on the one hand, and an established group of heterodox economists* (including many development economists and economic historians*) on the other.

The experience of the 1990s resulted in increasing criticism of the Washington Consensus by the start of the new millennium. During this time, major economies in Latin America, East Asia, and eastern Europe were all plunging into economic recession in spite of the fact that most of them had faithfully implemented neoliberal policy reform at the behest of the IFIs. A watershed moment in the debate occurred in 2000, when Joseph Stiglitz* was fired from his position as the World Bank's chief economist because of his increasingly vocal disagreement with the organization's neoliberal policies.

Chang's own experiences as a South Korean schooled in heterodox (non-mainstream) development economics gave him a personal connection to the growing disenchantment with the Washington

Consensus. With his own economic views shaped by the experience of South Korea's dramatic economic growth from the 1960s, Chang sought to apply economic history as a means of influencing the debate between neoliberal thinkers and development economists.

NOTES

1   Ha-Joon Chang, *Kicking Away the Ladder: Development Strategy in Historical Perspective* (London: Anthem Press, 2003), 2.

2   Walt Rostow, *The Stages of Economic Growth* (Cambridge: Cambridge University Press, 1960).

3   Simon Kuznets, *Toward a Theory of Economic Growth: With Reflections on the Economic Growth of Modern Nations* (London: Norton, 1968).

4   W. Arthur Lewis, *The Theory of Economic Growth* (Chicago, IL: R. D. Irwin, 1955).

5   Adam Smith, *An Inquiry into the Nature and Causes of the Wealth of Nations* (London: W. Strahan & T. Cadell, 1776).

6   Chang, *Kicking Away the Ladder*, 3.

7   Chang, *Kicking Away the Ladder*, 25.

THE AUTHOR'S CONTRIBUTION

KEY POINTS

- Chang uses the evidence of history to assess the practical and moral validity of current economic policies.

- In *Kicking Away the Ladder*, Ha-Joon Chang uses the economic history* of rich now-developed countries* (NDCs) to show that neoliberal* policies are not an effective means to allow less-developed countries* (LDCs) to achieve the benefits of development, such as prosperity and high living standards.

- *Kicking Away the Ladder* builds on the observations and ideas of other economists and economic historians, synthesizing them into a short, readable book.

Author's Aims

Ha-Joon Chang's *Kicking Away the Ladder: Development Strategy in Historical Perspective* is intended to give an informed voice to widespread discontent with the neoliberal economic policies that define the Washington Consensus,* using lessons from economic history. To that end, the book has three primary aims.

First, and most importantly, it seeks to show that during the early stages of their own economic growth* and development,* today's developed countries* did not practice the economic policies that they now recommend.

Second, the book questions the effectiveness of neoliberal policies* and institutions* in stimulating development; in this sense, an institution might be a tariff (tax) charged on imports and exports; a policy might be a decision to raise or lower that tariff. Chang outlines the theoretical basis for the opposition of many development

> ❝ There have been surprisingly few attempts to apply lessons learned from the historical experiences of developing countries to problems of contemporary development. ❞
>
> Ha-Joon Chang, *Kicking Away the Ladder: Development Strategy in Historical Perspective*

economists* to neoliberalism, presenting evidence from economic historians supporting a different approach. He shows that there is no reason to believe that neoliberalism is more effective in promoting growth than what has historically been proven to work.

The final aim of the book, and an extension of its first two aims, is to demonstrate that the current practices of international financial institutions* (IFIs) such as the World Bank* and the International Monetary Fund* (IMF) must be radically overhauled.

Kicking Away the Ladder offers a unique contribution to the standard methodology of the discipline of development economics. The book emphasizes the importance of historical analysis in crafting current development strategy, urging policymakers in developing countries* to learn from history rather than turning to theoretical models or allowing purely domestic concerns to limit their actions.

Approach

Ha-Joon Chang's approach in *Kicking Away the Ladder* is different from that of other development economists. He adds historical and moral dimensions to the debate against the Washington Consensus, rather than limiting the scope of his arguments to economic theory or contemporary evidence.

While the incorporation of economic history into development economics is not new, academics having drawn on the two disciplines together throughout the twentieth century, development economists have generally limited their historical studies to the country or countries with which they are concerned. Chang's use of economic history in *Kicking Away the Ladder*, however, is unique in that it focuses on one set of countries—now-developed countries (NDCs)—to draw lessons for the present situation of a second set of countries— less-developed countries (LDCs).

The moral dimension of Chang's argument is similarly unique. *Kicking Away the Ladder* is not a neutral study of which development strategies are most effective. Implicit in its title, content, and tone, rather, is the belief that developing countries continue to be poor because they have in effect been denied the chance to implement those development strategies that would be the most effective. Chang's historical narrative and theoretical discussions in *Kicking Away the Ladder* cannot, therefore, be considered neutral.

Contribution in Context

In the introduction to *Kicking Away the Ladder*, Ha-Joon Chang explicitly recognizes that there is a broader academic context to the book's arguments. He writes that "there have been heated debates on whether … recommended policies and institutions are in fact appropriate for today's developing countries."[1] Many of the arguments and much of the historical evidence he uses to support his side of the debate, which is that these policies and institutions are not appropriate, are drawn from other economists and economic historians. Some of these figures, including Erik Reinert,* Gabriel Palma,* John Toye,* and Robert Rowthorn,* contributed directly to Chang's thesis in *Kicking Away the Ladder* by providing insights and suggestions drawn from their own expertise. The book's titular hypothesis, namely that rich countries are "kicking away the ladder," is taken directly from the observations of the German American economist Friedrich List.*

Chang's evidence is drawn from the research of his contemporaries. His point that "throughout the nineteenth century and up until the

1920s, the USA was the fastest growing economy in the world, despite being the most protectionist during almost all of this period"[2] was taken from a 1993 publication by the economic historian Paul Bairoch* that systematically dismantles many of the myths of world economic history.[3] Chang's text is especially notable in synthesizing a number of widely held positions among development and heterodox economists* and encapsulating them in a short, accessible volume.

NOTES

1 Ha-Joon Chang, *Kicking Away the Ladder: Development Strategy in Historical Perspective* (London: Anthem Press, 2003), 5.

2 Chang, *Kicking Away the Ladder*, 30.

3 Paul Bairoch, *Economics and World History: Myths and Paradoxes* (Chicago, IL: University of Chicago Press, 1993).

SECTION 2
IDEAS

MAIN IDEAS

KEY POINTS

- Ha-Joon Chang's *Kicking Away the Ladder* focuses on the lack of evidence that economic policies* and institutions* recommended to developing countries* by the developed world are, in practice, effective.

- Chang demonstrates that, when they were developing, today's developed countries* relied on policies and institutions that are contrary to what they currently preach.

- *Kicking Away the Ladder* is written in a style accessible to a wide range of audiences, from policymakers to the general public.

Key Themes

Ha-Joon Chang's *Kicking Away the Ladder: Development Strategy in Historical Perspective* is centered on the hypocrisy within the global system concerning topics fundamental to the field of development:* economic policies and institutions. Each of these two topics is the subject of a chapter in *Kicking Away the Ladder*. Policies and institutions are closely related concepts, and the distinction between them is "necessarily arbitrary."[1] "Institutions," Chang writes, "are more permanent arrangements while policies are more easily changeable."[2] For instance, a tariff* (a tax on imports or exports) is an institution; the decision to raise or lower a tariff is an example of a policy.

Chang proceeds from the premise that today's rich countries— "now-developed countries"* (NDCs)—and international financial institutions* (IFIs) prescribe a certain set of policies and institutions to poor countries, supposedly to help the latter develop. These policies

> **“ It is time to think again about which policies and institutions will help today's developing countries to develop faster. ”**
>
> Ha-Joon Chang, *Kicking Away the Ladder: Development Strategy in Historical Perspective*

and institutions are all derived from neoliberalism* (a belief in the economic effectiveness of free markets and minimum state intervention). The book makes the overall point that the effectiveness of neoliberal policies and institutions is not supported by evidence. NDCs not only disregarded neoliberalism when they were growing economically but actively employed contrary methods. The overarching argument of *Kicking Away the Ladder*, explored through the topics of policies and institutions, is the notion that the global economic order is rigged in a way that prevents developing countries from catching up with their wealthier counterparts.

Exploring the Ideas

Kicking Away the Ladder consists of four chapters. The first is introductory, outlining the rationale behind Chang's work and laying out the premise and methodology: that the developed world "and the international development policy establishment that it controls"[3] pressure developing countries to adopt a certain set of "good policies" and "good institutions,"* as Chang refers to them, to stimulate economic development. These policies and institutions, generally known as the Washington Consensus,* are neoliberal in nature. *Kicking Away the Ladder* wades into "heated debates on whether or not these policies and institutions are in fact appropriate for today's developing countries."[4]

Chang demonstrates their inappropriateness by examining how today's developed countries themselves developed. His findings include "various elements of historical information which contradict the orthodox view of the history of capitalism"*—the exercise of trade and investment for private profit—and demonstrate that developed countries did not develop using the methods outlined in the Washington Consensus. Chang's conclusions led him further to ask "whether the developed countries are somehow trying to hide 'the secrets of their success'."[5]

The first of the book's two main ideas concerns policy. Chang suggests that what the developed world recommends to developing countries as "good policy" is in fact harmful for development. In the neoliberal view, a government's industrial trade and technology (ITT) policy should minimize interference with the free market.* This means avoiding state subsidies* and other forms of government assistance for the manufacturing sector, as well as pursuing a policy of free trade* and avoiding protectionism* (the economic policy of imposing taxes or regulations to restrict international trade, to the benefit of the nation imposing them).

According to Chang, the evidence from the history of developed countries contradicts the neoliberal consensus. "In most of these countries," Chang writes, "the policies that were used are almost the opposite of what the present orthodoxy says they employed and currently recommends that the currently developing countries also use."[6] Britain achieved "the technological lead that enabled [its] shift to a free trade regime … behind high and long-lasting tariff barriers."[7] In the United States, the federal government heavily subsidized industrial research and development and the development of transportation infrastructure. Germany, France, the Netherlands, and Sweden all used combinations of protectionism and government support for their industrial bases to develop. Only Switzerland industrialized without protectionism, mainly because of the high costs of protectionism given the small size of its domestic market. Since World War II,* interventionist trade and industrial policies have played a crucial role in the economic successes of Japan and other East Asian countries.

The second of Chang's main ideas concerns institutions. Chang examines various institutions recommended to developing countries by developed countries, including democracy,* an independent judiciary* (courts and judges), property rights,* corporate governance,* financial institutions, social welfare* (protection for a society's most vulnerable citizens), and labor institutions* (rules and practices that protect the rights and well-being of workers). He concludes that for the most part these "good institutions" were not crucial to the development of today's developed countries. In fact, they are the result of industrial trade and technology policy and other forms of state intervention. "That is *not* to say," Chang notes, "that developing countries should not adopt the institutions which currently prevail in developed countries … However, the benefits of institutional catch-up should not be exaggerated, as not all 'global standard' institutions are beneficial or necessary for all developing countries."[8]

Language and Expression

The accessible nature of Ha-Joon Chang's writing is a significant factor in *Kicking Away the Ladder*'s commercial success. Chang's arguments involve challenging economic concepts such as trade balances* and state subsidies. But almost no mathematics is used in its explanations. The result is a book easily understood by specialists and nonspecialists alike.

Chang's introductory chapter lays out a summary of the arguments proposed in his second and third chapters, which proceed logically and clearly with their own introductory and concluding sections, resummarizing their contents. Likewise, the final chapter consists of a further recap of the book's arguments. If this repetition perhaps renders elements of the book redundant, the reader is never lost.

Ultimately, *Kicking Away the Ladder* consists of two exercises. First, there is an analysis of the historical economic development of NDCs, which specifically examines policies and institutions. Second, these histories are then compared with the economic and institutional policies implemented by today's developing countries. As part of these exercises, Chang provides a broad range of historical facts and anecdotes to back up his arguments. He then deploys the information he has gathered to make the overall point that developing countries are currently being misled by developed countries, via the Washington Consensus, and told in effect, "Do as I say, not as I do."

NOTES

1   Ha-Joon Chang, *Kicking Away the Ladder: Development Strategy in Historical Perspective* (London: Anthem Press, 2003), 9.

2   Chang, *Kicking Away the Ladder*, 9.

3   Chang, *Kicking Away the Ladder*, 1.

4   Chang, *Kicking Away the Ladder*, 1.

5   Chang, *Kicking Away the Ladder*, 2.

6   Chang, *Kicking Away the Ladder*, 19.

7   Chang, *Kicking Away the Ladder*, 24.

8   Chang, *Kicking Away the Ladder*, 11.

MODULE 6
SECONDARY IDEAS

KEY POINTS

- In addition to its main arguments, *Kicking Away the Ladder* advocates the broader idea that the generally accepted narrative of capitalism,* trade, and development* is flawed.

- Chang challenges the standard history of capitalism's role in the successful economic development of the world's most powerful countries, and shows that not all "good institutions"* (democracy,* an independent judiciary,* social welfare,* and so on) are a prerequisite to growth.

- Chang's ideas about institutions* were not as widely scrutinized as his ideas on policies.*

Other Ideas

The broader secondary theme running through Ha-Joon Chang's *Kicking Away the Ladder: Development Strategy in Historical Perspective* is that official narratives on capitalism, trade, and development have limitations that must be exposed and challenged. This involves addressing several ideas within economics and economic history.*

Chang offers, for example, a narrative of the economic supremacy of Britain and, later, the United States that directly challenges orthodox readings and understandings. He shows that these places were not the bastions of laissez-faire economics* that they are often made out to have been (under "laissez-faire" economic policy, business is conducted with the most minimal government intervention and regulation). In doing so, Chang challenges the idea that free trade* and even capitalism in general resulted in enormous developmental success.

> **❝ The official historians of capitalism have been very
> successful in re-writing its history. ❞**
> Ha-Joon Chang, "Kicking Away the Ladder," *Post-Autistic Economics
> Review*

Chang also offers a unique perspective on institutions, challenging a number of widely held ideas on institutional development. For example, he makes clear that today's developed countries* established "good institutions" much later than previously thought. Furthermore, these institutions did not come about before far more important factors in economic growth were already present. Importantly, Chang also challenges the mainstream belief that "without patents and other private intellectual property rights,* [today's developed countries] would not have been able to generate the technologies that made them prosperous."[1]

The book demonstrates that traditional explanations about the historical relationship between free trade, capitalism, and economic development are based on certain key assumptions that can be overturned by contradictory facts; *Kicking Away the Ladder*, then, both questions the supposed benefits of neoliberalism* and challenges otherwise mainstream explanations of economic history.

Exploring the Ideas

At the start of *Kicking Away the Ladder*, Chang notes that, oddly, many of the critics of the Washington Consensus*—that is, the belief in the values of neoliberalism—"nevertheless take it for granted that these 'good policies' and '[good] institutions' were used by developed countries when they themselves were in the process of developing."[2] In its examination of the historical evidence surrounding the effectiveness of policies and institutions for development, the book finds this assumption to be incorrect. The implication is that mainstream narratives on economic development, which include the role of capitalism and free trade within it, are mistaken—possibly even willfully.

In the first chapter, Chang outlines the official history of capitalism used to justify neoliberalism in development strategy. He writes that "it is generally accepted that Britain became the world's first industrial power because of its laissez-faire policy,"[3] and that the United States only grew powerful after abandoning protectionism.* Chang disproves both claims, showing that Britain implemented extreme protectionist measures until its industrial base was strong enough to compete in a free trade regime and that the United States was the fastest-growing economy in the world during its protectionist period in the nineteenth century. His conclusions challenge the traditional explanation of capitalism's dominance in today's economic policymaking: that the free market has proved to be the most effective tool in bringing about prosperity.

In his chapter on institutions, Chang challenges the mainstream view on the role of institutions in economic development that "good institutions" are crucial to growth. Chang uses the United States as a case study, and shows that economic growth there occurred in parallel with a political system plagued by major flaws in its democracy. American politics during the nineteenth century, Chang writes, was characterized by a "spoils system" in which offices were allocated to supporters of the ruling party, as well as "widespread nepotism"* (the awarding of positions to relatives and friends) and other forms of corruption.[4]

In another challenge to the conventional wisdom on institutions, Chang addresses intellectual property rights and patent law. Institutional economists* believe "that the stronger the protection of property rights, the better it is for economic development, as such protection encourages the creation of wealth."[5] While patent laws were adopted by most of today's rich countries at some point in the eighteenth or nineteenth centuries, "even the most developed NDCs [now-developed countries*] were still routinely violating the IPR [intellectual property rights] of other countries' citizens well into the twentieth century."[6] Switzerland, for example, resisted implementation of a broad patent law until 1907.[7]

For Chang, the lack of protection for intellectual property* would have been beneficial to the economic development of these countries. He cites the principle that merely because some groups, whether individuals or organizations, own intellectual property, this does not necessarily mean they are able to exploit it effectively; others may be more efficient in its use. In that case, society should allow the latter rights to that property.[8]

Overlooked

Kicking Away the Ladder's initial critics focused mainly on Chang's arguments concerning state intervention and protectionism. The book's chapter on institutions, arguing that neoliberal institutions are not necessarily a prerequisite to economic development—received less attention. The well-known and comprehensive critique of Chang's ideas on institutions by the American economist Douglas Irwin,* for example, was limited to criticisms of Chang's definitions and his implication that historical lessons about institutions could be applied today.[9] The work's historical facts were not in dispute.

Chang makes another innovative, though often overlooked argument, in his chapter on institutions, arguing that government corruption was widespread during periods of rapid economic development in the United States and Europe.[10] The implications of this argument run counter to the mainstream view of economists and policymakers that eliminating corruption is a crucial part of successful economic development.[11] If the history presented in *Kicking Away the Ladder* is accurate, it could have important implications for anticorruption programs in developing countries* funded by rich countries' development aid budgets. Chang's critics have, however, given little attention to this aspect of the book.

NOTES

1   Ha-Joon Chang, *Kicking Away the Ladder: Development Strategy in Historical Perspective* (London: Anthem Press House, 2003), 2.

2   Chang, *Kicking Away the Ladder*, 1.

3   Chang, *Kicking Away the Ladder*, 1.

4   Chang, *Kicking Away the Ladder*, 78–9.

5   Chang, *Kicking Away the Ladder*, 82.

6   Chang, *Kicking Away the Ladder*, 85.

7   Chang, *Kicking Away the Ladder*, 85.

8   Chang, *Kicking Away the Ladder*, 83.

9   Douglas Irwin, "Book Review of Kicking Away the Ladder by Ha-Joon Chang," *EH.NET*, April 2004, accessed January 12, 2016, http://eh.net/book_reviews/kicking-away-the-ladder-development-strategy-in-historical-perspective.

10 Chang, *Kicking Away the Ladder*, 78–9.

11 Geoffrey Hodgson and Shuxia Jiang, "The Economics of Corruption and the Corruption of Economics," *Journal of Economic Issues* 41, no. 4 (2007).

MODULE 7
ACHIEVEMENT

KEY POINTS

- Using a clearly defined historical analysis, *Kicking Away the Ladder* offers original arguments against the conventional wisdom on development* strategy.

- The book introduced a historical perspective into the debate about development policy shortly after the developing world experienced severe economic crises in the late 1990s.

- In its historical approach, *Kicking Away the Ladder* fails to address how policies* and institutions* that worked in the past can be implemented today.

Assessing the Argument

Ha-Joon Chang's argument in *Kicking Away the Ladder: Development Strategy in Historical Perspective* can be assessed on the basis of how well it supports his aims.

The Washington Consensus* is a set of neoliberal* economic policies recommended to developing countries* by international financial institutions* as a means to encourage economic growth;* inventively, Chang aims to challenge the belief that these policies are effective through a focus on rich now-developed countries* (NDCs) rather than on poorer, developing nations.

Chang's arguments regarding institutions are meant to provide a different direction to that offered by existing debates in the field. Understanding the historical lessons of the development of institutions in richer countries, he claims, allows developing countries the obvious benefit of hindsight. In this way, Chang's chapters on institutions and

> **❝ A provocative critique of mainstream economists'
> sermons directed to developing countries, [*Kicking Away
> the Ladder*] demands attention.❞**
>
> Charles Kindleberger, book jacket of *Kicking Away the Ladder:
> Development Strategy in Historical Perspective*

polices share the same method of research and analysis.

Achievement in Context

Ha-Joon Chang wrote *Kicking Away the Ladder* in the wake of serious
economic crises in Southeast Asia (1997), eastern Europe (1997–9),
and South America (2000–1). These events raised fundamental
questions about the effectiveness of the Washington Consensus and
neoliberal economics. For example, the 1999 meeting in Seattle of the
World Trade Organization*—an organization that seeks to promote
international trade through the elimination of restrictions and taxes—
experienced the largest protests and public backlash in the institution's
history. The academic context at the time was shaped by debates
stemming from the 1980s, in which neoliberals and an emerging
group of heterodox* (contrary to the mainstream) economists
disagreed over the implications of competing economic theories for
developing countries.

The publication of *Kicking Away the Ladder* represented a
breakthrough, shifting the focus of the debate toward history rather
than theory, and toward developed countries* rather than developing
countries. These were innovations that many necessarily considered
highly provocative. For neoliberal economists, for example, the
historical assumptions on which much of their credibility depended
were undermined. In the same way, for development economists,* the
book represented a criticism of their methodology and research focus.

Limitations

Kicking Away the Ladder's unique historical approach is both a notable achievement and the source of some of the book's limitations. While Chang specifically intended to evaluate the usefulness of certain policies and institutions in development strategy, he bases this evaluation on the experience of today's rich countries decades or even centuries ago. Translating their histories into today's global economic landscape is not always either easy or helpful. Consequently, *Kicking Away the Ladder* promises the reader a study of development strategy to counter the policy prescriptions of neoliberals when, in reality, it offers a study of economic history;* applying its arguments to the complex situations faced by developing countries today is rarely straightforward.

For example, one of the biggest problems with the current practice of prescribing "good institutions"* to developing countries is "the difficulty of institutional transplantation" and "the attempt to impose a common institutional standard on countries with different conditions"[1]—the expectation that an institution transplanted from one national context will simply operate in a similar fashion in another national context. Chang suggests that developing countries should instead learn from history, presenting a historical analysis of how institutions evolved in developed nations as the most helpful approach. Yet he fails to address the problem that, precisely because of the inappropriateness of imposing common institutional standards across different environments, the experience of developed nations, which are completely different politically, geographically, and culturally from today's developing countries, may not always be particularly relevant.

NOTES

1   Ha-Joon Chang, *Kicking Away the Ladder: Development Strategy in Historical Perspective* (London: Anthem Press, 2003), 70.

MODULE 8
PLACE IN THE AUTHOR'S WORK

KEY POINTS

- *Kicking Away the Ladder*, one of Ha-Joon Chang's earliest books, was an important step in developing some of his best-known ideas.

- The book brings together several important themes from Chang's early research into a clear argument against forcing free trade* and neoliberal* ideas on developing countries.*

- It similarly bestowed a high profile on Chang, establishing him as one of the leading thinkers in development economics* today.

Positioning

As a student, much of Ha-Joon Chang's academic study and research was focused on microeconomic* issues—that is, questions about the economic behavior of individuals—related to intellectual property* and industrial policy.* Nonetheless, he has been active in debates surrounding macroeconomics*—how economies as a whole behave— since the start of his teaching career in 1990.

One of Chang's earliest papers on development economics anticipated the ideas he would put forward in *Kicking Away the Ladder: Development Strategy in Historical Perspective* 10 years later. A 1993 article, "The Political Economy* of Industrial Policy in Korea," argues that explanations of Korea's rapid economic development after World War II* "which try to dismiss the role of the Korean state in the developmental process have a weak theoretical and empirical basis."[1] In other words, state-led development was crucial to the South Korean

> **❝ Let's make economics accessible to people and let them judge. ❞**
> Ha-Joon Chang, *Byline*

economic success.

Exploring alternative narratives of economic development to the free market* doctrines of the Washington Consensus* has, therefore, long been one of Chang's main priorities as a scholar. *Kicking Away the Ladder*, only his second book, represents an important step in bringing his ideas on the subject into the academic mainstream. Most importantly, it served as a foundation on which Chang further developed these ideas in his later books, *Bad Samaritans: The Myth of Free Trade and the Secret History of Capitalism* (2008),[2] and *23 Things They Don't Tell You About Capitalism* (2010).[3] Both books cover similar themes to *Kicking Away the Ladder* (although they are over twice the length).

Integration

As a book highlighting the importance of state intervention in stimulating economic growth, *Kicking Away the Ladder* fits well into Chang's overall intellectual background. The book incorporates several themes from his earlier academic work, such as protectionism* through tariffs* and state subsidies* (cash assistance given by a nation's government to groups or businesses), controls on foreign direct investment* (investments in a private business by a foreign person or entity), corporate governance* (rules concerning the ways in which businesses must operate), intellectual property,* and the social welfare* system.

It also offers two important points of departure from Chang's past work, however. First, it bases the counterargument against neoliberalism in economic history* rather than contemporary empirical evidence (that is, evidence that can be verified by observation). Second, although it is written for the benefit of developing countries, the book focuses primarily on Western, developed countries.*

The greatest coherence within the collection of books written by Chang occurs between *Kicking Away the Ladder* and its intellectual successors *Bad Samaritans* and *23 Things*. It is clear that *Kicking Away the Ladder* was the launch pad for these more recent works, which repackage its core ideas in an even more accessible manner aimed at the widest possible readership. *Bad Samaritans* focuses on and fleshes out one of the key arguments from *Kicking Away the Ladder*, which is that free trade is not the best policy* for development. *23 Things* is concerned with Chang's broader criticisms of neoliberalism and free-market institutions.*

Significance

When *Kicking Away the Ladder* was published in 2003, Chang was already a highly respected academic, serving as assistant director of the Department of Development Studies at Cambridge University. Yet whatever the importance of his later books, *Kicking Away the Ladder* is in many ways Chang's most significant work—not least as it was the first of his books to receive public attention outside academia. The book received the 2003 Gunnar Myrdal Prize from the European Association for Evolutionary Political Economy,[4] and was cited as one of the reasons why Chang went on to win the Wassily Leontief Prize awarded by Tufts University for Advancing the Frontiers of Economic Thought in 2005.[5]

Beyond the attention it brought its author, *Kicking Away the Ladder* is also notable for creating a strand in development thought that revives arguments from early twentieth-century development economics and evidence from history to counter modern arguments for free trade and neoliberal policy. This position was developed further in *Bad Samaritans*, carving a space within the discipline for Chang to become its leading exponent.

NOTES

1   Ha-Joon Chang, "The Political Economy of Industrial Policy in Korea," *Cambridge Journal of Economics* 17 (1993).

2   Ha-Joon Chang, *Bad Samaritans: The Myth of Free Trade and the Secret History of Capitalism* (New York: Bloomsbury Press, 2008).

3   Ha-Joon Chang, *23 Things They Don't Tell You About Capitalism* (New York: Bloomsbury Press, 2010).

4   Kyung-Sup Chang, Ben Fine, and Linda Weiss, eds., *Developmental Politics in Transition: The Neoliberal Era and Beyond* (London: Palgrave Macmillan, 2012), xiv.

5   See Neva R. Goodwin, "Leontief Prize 2005: Ha-Joon Chang." Speech, 2005 Leontief Prize Award Presentation, October 27, 2005.

SECTION 3
IMPACT

MODULE 9
THE FIRST RESPONSES

KEY POINTS

- Early critiques of Ha-Joon Chang's *Kicking Away the Ladder* attacked the rigor of the book's historical analysis and its methodology.

- Chang responded to his critics by further developing his ideas and presenting them in a later book, *Bad Samaritans*.

- Chang's arguments in *Kicking Away the Ladder* continue to be debated as a result of their inclusion in subsequent books and relevance to current events.

Criticism

The most detailed of the early criticisms of Ha-Joon Chang's *Kicking Away the Ladder: Development Strategy in Historical Perspective* came from the economist Douglas Irwin.* It focused on what Irwin saw as weaknesses in the book's historical analysis and methodology, where "the biggest disappointment … is Ha-Joon Chang's extremely superficial treatment of the historical experiences of the now developed countries."*[1]

Irwin's first questions address the analysis behind Chang's claim that "infant industry promotion (but not just tariff* protection,* I hasten to add) has been the key to the development* of most nations."[2] He argues that Chang does not prove a direct relationship between the promotion of young industries and economic development. The fact that economies grew under industry promotion policies "does not mean that the outcome can be attributed to those specific policies."[3] Countries like the United States, Irwin argues, are likely to have

> **❝** Someone asked, 'Who is the most exciting thinker the profession has turned out in the last 15 years?' Several of us spoke up at once—'Ha-Joon Chang!' **❞**
>
> Dr. Neva R. Goodwin, 2005 Leontief Prize Award Ceremony

developed *in spite of* protectionist policies in the nineteenth century as a result of its favorable demographic and political conditions.[4]

Irwin then points out that Chang's method of research and analysis suffers from selection bias—it is an analysis based on examples that can only prove his reading correct; his historical evidence is only taken from countries that developed economically during the nineteenth century and a small sample of the policies they employed. By neglecting to examine countries that *failed* to develop and investigating whether they pursued the same policies, Chang's book uses "a poor scientific and historical method."[5]

Responses

The dialogue between Chang and his critics was continued over several years after the publication of *Kicking Away the Ladder.* Chang's response to early criticisms was to research and expand his ideas further. In his 2008 book *Bad Samaritans*, Chang addresses one of Douglas Irwin's concerns by examining the cases of countries that failed to develop and arguing that they had largely followed neoliberal* policies.* While his studies of these countries are not as detailed as those of now-developed countries in *Kicking Away the Ladder*, Chang writes that "Mexico is a particularly striking example of the failure of premature wholesale trade liberalization, but there are other examples."[6] He goes on to list the cases of Ivory Coast, Zimbabwe, and others.[7]

Chang also uses *Bad Samaritans* to address Irwin's criticism about confusing correlation and causation (the idea that events that appear to show some kind of association can be understood as fundamentally linked). While economists such as Irwin argue that countries like the United States grew despite protectionism, rather than because of it, "[the] force of this counter-argument," Chang writes, "is diminished by the fact that, as we shall see, many other countries with few of those conditions also grew rapidly behind protective barriers. Germany, Sweden, France, Finland, Austria, Japan, Taiwan and Korea come to mind."[8]

Conflict and Consensus

Chang's arguments in *Kicking Away the Ladder* continue to receive attention in the debates surrounding development today, especially after the global financial crisis* of 2008. Chang's expansion of his arguments in subsequent books also meant that critics could continue to engage with the work. Consequently, conflict with Chang's ideas continues.

Tellingly, in a review of *Kicking Away the Ladder* written 10 years after the book's publication, the University of York researcher Seb Bytyci* repeated several criticisms similar to those posed by Irwin in 2004; for him, Chang fails to show "why alternative theories are not satisfactory to explain the historical development of the NDC [now-developed country]."[9]

Bytyci also repeats Irwin's point that the book does not give any cases of countries that failed to develop while the rich nations developed, which would have allowed a clear comparison of their policies. Even in *Bad Samaritan*, Chang's cases of countries that failed to develop while using neoliberal policies were taken from the twentieth century, which presented a different global political and economic environment from that of the nineteenth century, the focus of *Kicking Away the Ladder*. However, Bytici concludes that "these shortcomings do not diminish the value of the book. It is a great contribution … and will continue to influence the debate on development."[10]

NOTES

1 Douglas Irwin, "Book Review of Kicking Away the Ladder by Ha-Joon Chang," *EH.NET*, April 2004, accessed January 12, 2016, http://eh.net/book_reviews/kicking-away-the-ladder-development-strategy-in-historical-perspective.

2 Ha-Joon Chang, *Kicking Away the Ladder: Development Strategy in Historical Perspective* (London: Anthem Press, 2003), 10.

3 Irwin, "Book Review."

4 Irwin, "Book Review."

5 Irwin, "Book Review."

6 Ha-Joon Chang, *Bad Samaritans: The Myth of Free Trade and the Secret History of Capitalism* (New York: Bloomsbury Press, 2008), 53.

7 Chang, *Bad Samaritans*, 53.

8 Chang, *Bad Samaritans*, 39.

9 Seb Bytyci, "Review—Kicking Away the Ladder: Development Strategy in Historical Perspective," *ID: International Dialogue, a Multidisciplinary Journal of World Affairs* 3 (2013): 185.

10 Bytyci, "Review," 186.

MODULE 10
THE EVOLVING DEBATE

KEY POINTS

- Ha-Joon Chang's *Kicking Away the Ladder* has found a wide audience among academics and policymakers alike who deal with development* challenges.

- While the book did not establish a new school of thought, it led to Chang becoming a leader in the school of thought that favors state interventionism in development.

- *Kicking Away the Ladder* continues to feature in a great deal of current scholarship.

Uses and Problems

Ha-Joon Chang's *Kicking Away the Ladder: Development Strategy in Historical Perspective* was aimed directly at decisionmakers responsible for developing countries.* In this respect, the book's ideas were widely influential. Chang has worked as a consultant in several international development programs and has frequently advised United Nations* and government officials. Most notably, Rafael Correa,* president of Ecuador, has cited Chang as a direct influence in his own views on economics.[1] In 2009, Chang was invited to address the African Development Bank* (an international financial institution* aimed at encouraging economic development in Africa). In this address, he presented many of his arguments and data from *Kicking Away the Ladder*.[2]

Kicking Away the Ladder's arguments have also been carried forward by Justin Yifu Lin*—once chief economist of the World Bank,* an organization that the work heavily criticizes. Lin's book *The Quest for Prosperity*, written while he was still chief economist and published in

> ** ❝ How has this wonderful subject we call economics become so narrow-minded? I find that really sad. ❞ **
> Ha-Joon Chang, *Financial Times*

2012, examines the economic histories of today's developed countries*
in order to draw lessons about how developing countries can help
themselves. *The Quest for Prosperity* cites Chang several times,[3] and uses
the same general methodological framework as *Kicking Away the
Ladder*, even if it aims to make a slightly different point.

Schools of Thought

While Chang did not initiate a new school of thought in *Kicking Away
the Ladder*, the book nonetheless reignited the arguments against
neoliberalism* by framing the debate in terms of empirical evidence
from developed countries. One of the book's central propositions, that
governments are required to play an important role in the regulation
and maintenance of their economies, was argued in the nineteenth
century by the German political philosopher Karl Marx* and in the
twentieth century by the influential economists John Maynard
Keynes* and Karl Polanyi.* As Chang notes, protection for young,
developing industries has also been advocated by economists since
Alexander Hamilton* (first Secretary of the United States Treasury)
and the German American Friedrich List* in the eighteenth century.
Chang also states in the introduction that some of the founders of
development economics* (including Polanyi, Walt Rostow,* and
Simon Kuznets*) relied on studies of history to test the assumptions of
the discipline.

Chang, however, has taken on the mantle of many of these thinkers
and has become the leading figure in arguing for state intervention in
development today. In *A History of Development Economics Thought*, the
economist Shahrukh Rafi Khan* writes that *Kicking Away the Ladder*

is "the most prominent" work in a strand of development literature concerned with protectionism* and state intervention in economic activities by today's developed countries in the past.[4]

In Current Scholarship

Despite its relatively recent publication and the fact that it draws mainly on existing arguments, Chang's *Kicking Away the Ladder* has been remarkably influential in current scholarship. The book is frequently mentioned in textbooks on development economics, including Richard Peet and Elaine Hartwick's *Theories of Development* (2015), as a notable example of criticism of neoliberalism.[5] In short, *Kicking Away the Ladder* has grown from a radical work of popular economics to a seminal text in development thought.

Much of the scholarship that draws on *Kicking Away the Ladder* is, naturally, critical of free trade* policies. However, Chang's ideas have been cited in works that deal with other aspects of development economics as well; an example is a 2014 paper by Joseph Stiglitz,* chief economist of the World Bank from 1997 to 2000, in which he argues that the pace of a country's innovation is related to the level of investment* the state makes in innovation. Furthermore, Stiglitz cites *Kicking Away the Ladder*'s evidence that the institution* of intellectual property rights* does not need to be strong in order for innovation to take place.[6] Stiglitz makes clear that Chang's ideas on institutions are as influential in current scholarship as his thoughts on free trade.

NOTES

1   Rafael Correa, "Presentación del libro 'El rostro oculto del TLC,'" *La Insignia*, May 20, 2006.

2   Ha-Joon Chang, "Economic History of the Developed World: Lessons for Africa," Lecture, Eminent Speakers Program of the African Development Bank, February 26, 2009.

3   Justin Yifu Lin, *The Quest for Prosperity: How Developing Economies Can*

Take Off (Princeton, NJ: Princeton University Press, 2012), 98, 148, 248.

4   Shahrukh Rafi Khan, *A History of Development Economics Thought: Challenges and Counter-challenges* (New York: Routledge, 2014), 122.

5   Richard Peet and Elaine Hartwick, *Theories of Development: Contentions, Arguments, Alternatives* (3rd Ed.) (New York: Guilford Press, 2015), 76.

6   Joseph E. Stiglitz, "Intellectual Property Rights, the Pool of Knowledge, and Innovation," NBER Working Paper 20014 (March 2014): 2.

MODULE 11
IMPACT AND INFLUENCE TODAY

KEY POINTS

- Published shortly after a series of economic crises in developing countries,* Ha-Joon Chang's *Kicking Away the Ladder* was instrumental in reinforcing growing criticism of neoliberalism.*

- The book's ideas were expanded upon, updated, and addressed by critics as Chang published later works.

- While Chang's critics have been academics and policymakers alike, his ideas have been influential in both communities.

Position

When *Kicking Away the Ladder: Development Strategy in Historical Perspective* was published in 2003, developing countries were just coming out of a period, the late 1990s, characterized by economic crises associated with the application of neoliberal policies. Within a decade, the world would see two more major crises, the global financial crisis* of 2008 (a crisis with its roots in the practices of certain US banks and financial institutions) and, shortly afterwards, the European debt crisis* (a crisis in which certain European nations found themselves troubled by unsustainable levels of debt). Both further shook the public's faith in free market* fundamentalism.

As the first major example of Chang's prominent criticisms of unrestrained capitalism* today, *Kicking Away the Ladder* has consistently played an important role since these seismic economic events. Chang has continued to reiterate the importance of government spending in protecting industrial sectors and has attacked the adoption of neoliberal

> ❝ The best economists are those who look around at
> our man-made world and ask themselves 'why'? Chang
> is one such. ❞
>
> Sean O'Grady, *Independent*

policies such as cuts in spending on welfare programs and infrastructure
to reduce deficits (roughly, the gap between a nation's income and its
spending). Both of these are fundamental themes in *Kicking Away the
Ladder*. "During the 1982 developing world debt crisis, the 1994
Mexican crisis, the 1997 Asian crisis, the Brazilian and the Russian
crises in 1998, and the Argentinian crisis of 2002," Chang wrote in
2012, "all the crises-stricken countries were forced (usually by the
IMF*) to cut spending and run budget surpluses, only to see their
economies sink deeper into recession."[1]

Interaction

Chang's later books, *Bad Samaritans* and *23 Things They Don't Tell You
About Capitalism*, were written as a means of developing further the
core arguments in *Kicking Away the Ladder* and updating them in
response to admirers and critics alike. Written after Chang had already
established himself as a leading critic of neoliberalism, these later
books received even more publicity and, consequently, more detailed
attention from critics.

The most comprehensive recent criticism of Chang's ideas came
in 2009 from the development economist William Easterly* in
response to the publication of *Bad Samaritans*. As with the economist
Douglas Irwin's* earlier review of *Kicking Away the Ladder*, Easterly
accuses Chang of making "outlandish claims" in favor of
protectionism* while being "unaware of both the perils of spurious
patterns and the failure of most previous research to establish truly
verifiable patterns for explaining growth."[2] In other words, Easterly

accuses Chang of relying on inadequate evidence to support his claims and failing to prove that the link between protectionism and economic growth* is causal—in other words, direct.

The Continuing Debate

Other critics, among them the economics journalist Martin Wolf* and the former World Bank chief economist Anne Kreuger,* have criticized Chang's apparent over-confidence in protectionist policies* like import substitution* (an economic policy aimed at building national self-reliance through the elimination of foreign imports and their replacement with domestic products). In a response to these criticisms, Chang has written, "I do not advocate 'across-the-board import substitution' … I go to a great length in [*Bad Samaritans*] to explain why trade is essential for economic development."[3] Chang's issue with trade is simply that *free* trade*—that is, unregulated trade— is inappropriate as a means of encouraging economic development.

Today, Chang's arguments exercise considerable influence among increasing numbers of policymakers. Put simply, politically, in many developing countries, Chang is winning the debate. The majority of Latin American countries, in particular, have drifted away from the neoliberalism imposed on them by the developed world and international financial institutions* (IFIs) in previous decades. Chang attributes this shift partly to the failures of neoliberalism and partly to the work of economists like himself. The recent global financial crisis of 2008, he has stated, will cause Latin American nations to "move away even further [from neoliberalism]."[4]

NOTES

1   Ha-Joon Chang, "Austerity Has Never Worked," *Guardian*, June 4, 2012, accessed February 3, 2016, http://www.theguardian.com/ commentisfree/2012/jun/04/austerity-policy-eurozone-crisis.

2   William Easterly, "The Anarchy of Success," *New York Review of Books* 56, no. 15 (2009).

3   Ha-Joon Chang, "Response to Martin Wolf's 'The Growth of Nations'," *Financial Times*, August 3, 2007, accessed January 12, 2016, http://www. cepr.net/documents/publications/FT_HaJoon.pdf.

4   "Economist Ha-Joon Chang on 'The Myth of Free Trade and the Secret History of Capitalism,'" *Democracy Now*, March 10, 2009, accessed November 10, 2015, http://www.democracynow.org/2009/3/10/economist_ ha_joon_chang_on_the.

MODULE 12
WHERE NEXT?

KEY POINTS

- Ha-Joon Chang's *Kicking Away the Ladder* has the potential to remain one of the most important works in the continuing debate on neoliberalism* in development* strategy.

- The book has inspired other academics to present alternative histories of development economics,* and has become influential among policymakers.

- *Kicking Away the Ladder* is a concise but wide-ranging account of the "real story" of how today's developed countries* became rich by practicing the opposite of what they now preach.

Potential

In many ways, Ha-Joon Chang's *Kicking Away the Ladder: Development Strategy in Historical Perspective* has been superseded in antineoliberal development literature by his later books. *Bad Samaritans* in particular, published in 2008, is essentially a more detailed, updated version of *Kicking Away the Ladder.* As such, it has largely taken the latter's place as the focal point of Chang's critics and disciples alike. Chang also uses *Bad Samaritans* as an opportunity to address some of *Kicking Away the Ladder*'s critics, such as the economist Douglas Irwin.*

Nonetheless, *Kicking Away the Ladder* will still be remembered as a classic. It is the book with which Chang, today one of the most respected economists in the world, made his name. Furthermore, it provides the core arguments of the main idea for which Chang has become known: that the neoliberal agenda and the supposed history on which it is based are essentially false and serve only to perpetuate

> **❝ The future of economics is ultimately a matter for all of us. ❞**
> Ha-Joon Chang, *Guardian*

underdevelopment.

It is an idea that will continue to remain in the public debate as long as there is discontent with neoliberalism's role in development economics. In the aftermath of the 2008 global financial crisis,* criticism of neoliberalism has only grown, its belief in unfettered free markets* increasingly linked with global inequality[1] and exploitation.[2] As the first popular and accessible book to challenge the historical narrative of neoliberalism, *Kicking Away the Ladder* is certain to remain a core text.

Future Directions

Since Chang wrote *Kicking Away the Ladder*, other economists and economic historians have emulated his approach. The Norwegian development economist Erik Reinert,* credited with providing historical sources for Chang in *Kicking Away the Ladder*, has been particularly prominent in presenting research on an alternative history of global development to the general public. In his book *How Rich Countries Got Rich and Why Poor Countries Stay Poor*, Reinert combines the historical narratives used by Chang with more theoretical and philosophical questions. Whereas Chang argues that free trade* was never key to successful development, Reinert goes further by challenging the morality behind free trade and exposes its role as a tool for economic exploitation of poor countries by rich countries.[3] As a specialist in economic history,* Reinert bridges many of the gaps between history and theory in a way that *Kicking Away the Ladder* did not.

Chang's work has also become influential among policymakers, including politicians and officials in developing countries* and in international organizations. Chang has been hired as a consultant and guest speaker at the World Bank* and by the United Nations Development Program.* In particular, he has been credited as a significant influence on Latin American policymakers. It is plain that in many ways the future application of his ideas will be in policymaking and the work of development practitioners. This accords precisely with the spirit of *Kicking Away the Ladder*, which is to stress observable and measurable real-world evidence in contrast to ideology and pure theory in development strategy.

Summary

Kicking Away the Ladder remains a key text in development economics studies. It disputes the dominant historical narrative in modern development policymaking circles that today's developed countries got rich by adopting neoliberal policies* and institutions*. Furthermore, the book criticizes the imposition (or the willing adoption) of those same policies and institutions as a means of development. These are important ideas in a world where deep and persistent inequalities between rich and poor nations, coupled with the apparent failure of neoliberal reforms in developing countries, have reignited dissatisfaction with the global economic order.

From the moment of its publication, *Kicking Away the Ladder* was a decisively new and influential contribution to development economics. The book builds a compelling case for overhauling development strategies for today's poor countries by examining the economic history of today's rich countries. Chang's methodology unites the conclusions of many economic historians with the theories of heterodox economists* in the service of development policymaking. The book's academic rigor, appeal to professionals, and accessible writing precisely underline its importance as a seminal work.

The wealth of historical information that Chang presents in

Kicking Away the Ladder builds into a series of compelling arguments. Chang gives well-sourced accounts of the economic histories of Great Britain, the United States, and various European countries in the period after the Industrial Revolution* in the nineteenth century. These countries are the main protagonists behind today's efforts to force developing countries to abandon protectionism* and state intervention in their national development strategies. Yet Chang's accounts demonstrate that it was exactly such protectionism and state intervention that were the key, however long ago, to making today's rich countries economically dominant.

Chang also makes an interesting case for rethinking the way developing countries should implement institutional reform. If neoliberal institutions such as free trade, minimal government control over the economy, and the dominance of private enterprise have some role at least to play in boosting the economic growth* and development of the world's poorest countries, they are far from prerequisites.

NOTES

1   George Monbiot, "If You Think We're Done with Neoliberalism, Think Again," *Guardian*, January 14, 2013, accessed February 3, 2016, http://www. theguardian.com/commentisfree/2013/jan/14/neoliberal-theory-economic-failure.

2   Claudia von Werlhof, "Neoliberal Globalization: Is there an Alternative to Plundering the Earth?" in *The Global Economic Crisis: The Great Depression of the XXI Century*, ed. Michel Chossudovsky and Andrew Gavin Marshall (Montreal: Global Research Publishers, 2010), 116–45.

3   Erik S. Reinert, *How Rich Countries Got Rich … and Why Poor Countries Stay Poor* (London: Constable & Robinson, 2007).

GLOSSARY

GLOSSARY OF TERMS

African Development Bank: an international financial institution aimed at encouraging economic development and well-being in Africa.

Capitalism: an economic system in which ownership of the resources and tools required for production and the ability to realize profits from property, goods, and services are in the hands of individual citizens and businesses.

Central planning: an economic system in which the government creates a comprehensive strategy to determine how resources are allocated.

Colonialism: the forced acquisition, settlement, and political or economic control of one territory by the political power of another territory.

Corporate governance: the administration of profitmaking companies on the basis of a clear set of rules.

Democracy: a system of government in which all citizens participate in decisionmaking, usually through voting.

Developed country: a sovereign state with an advanced economy and infrastructure that provides a high quality of life for its citizens.

Developing country: a sovereign state that has not yet advanced its economy and infrastructure to a level that provides a high quality of life for its citizens.

Development: the process by which a sovereign state advances its economy, infrastructure, and quality of life for its citizens.

Development economics: the study of economics related to increasing a country's overall wealth and the quality of life of its citizens.

Economic growth: an increase in a country's economic output and relative wealth.

Economic history: a discipline of the social sciences that studies the history and development of economies.

Economic liberalization: a process in which governments ease the regulations and restrictions affecting private activity in the economy.

Endogenous growth theory: the position held by some economists that forces within the economy, such as the knowledge and innovation of the population, are more significant to economic growth than external forces.

European debt crisis: an ongoing debt crisis within the European Union in which several member states have been unable to repay loans and private and public creditors.

First World: a general term that refers loosely to economically developed, industrialized, mostly Western nations.

Foreign direct investment: the purchase of controlling interest in a private business by a foreign person or entity.

Free market: an economic system characterized by parties engaging in exchange with minimal restriction and regulation.

Free trade: unrestricted exchange of goods or services between the citizens of different countries.

Global financial crisis (2008): the most serious financial crisis since the Great Depression of the 1930s. The crisis was caused by the collapse of the American housing bubble and resulted in mass defaults on debts, affecting financial institutions and markets worldwide.

Globalization: the process of increasing interconnectedness among global markets, politics, and cultures.

"Good institutions": the customs and organizations that, according to the consensus in the developed world, are required for a nation to develop. These include democracy, a judiciary (legal system) independent of outside influence, property rights (rules protecting the ownership of physical or intellectual property), corporate governance (the administration of profit-making companies on the basis of certain rules), financial institutions, social welfare (protections for the nation's most vulnerable), and labor institutions (rules and practices that protect the rights and wellbeing of workers).

Heterodox school of economics: theories, methodologies, and schools of thought in economics that exist outside the mainstream teachings of the discipline.

Human capital: a measure of the productive resources offered by an individual to the economy, including knowledge, abilities, skills, and creativity.

Import substitution: an economic policy aimed at building national self-reliance through the elimination of foreign imports and their replacement with domestic production.

Independent judiciary: the independence of those legal elements of a government—essentially courts and judges—charged with the impartial application of the law.

Industrial policy: a country's strategy to encourage economic growth through industrialization.

Industrial Revolution: an event in world history between 1760 and approximately 1840 in which national economies, primarily in the West, were transformed by widely adopting machines and automated manufacturing processes into the production of goods.

Industrialization: a process in which a society transforms from a rural, agricultural one to an industrial one, involving a major reorganization of the economy.

Institution: an established practice deeply rooted in a country's laws or culture. Courts, trade unions, and taxation policies are all examples of such institutions.

Institutional economics: a field of study concerned with understanding the role of institutions in the economy.

Intellectual property: inventions or concepts traceably derived from an individual's or entity's own creativity or ideas and which remain the legal property of such individuals or entities.

International financial institutions: organizations dedicated to providing economic support to governments in the form of expertise, grants, or loans for development activities.

International Monetary Fund (IMF): an international organization created in 1944 to foster global monetary cooperation by facilitating international trade and intervening in financial or monetary crises.

Investment: the act of purchasing an asset in order to derive profit from it at a later date.

Keynesian economics: an economic school of thought that teaches that in the short run a country's economic output is influenced by the economy's level of aggregate demand.

Korean War: a violent Cold War conflict between North Korea, backed by the communist Soviet Union and China, and South Korea, backed by the capitalist United States, fought between 1950 and 1953. It resulted in the division of Korea and the development of a communist North Korea and a capitalist South Korea.

Labor institutions: rules and practices that protect the rights and well-being of workers.

Laissez-faire economics: a policy of minimizing government involvement in economic affairs.

Less-developed country (LDC): a term used by Ha-Joon Chang to refer to countries that have not yet fully industrialized.

Macroeconomics: a branch of study in economics concerned with the economy as a whole.

Marxism: a view of the social sciences that analyzes political and economic events through the lens of relations between socioeconomic classes (the working class and the investing class, for example).

Microeconomics: a branch of study in economics concerned with the economic behavior of individuals.

Nepotism: a form of corruption in organizations in which superiors favor relatives and close friends.

Neoclassical economics: an approach to economics concerned with prices, outputs, and income distribution in an economy as the results of changes in the supply of and demand for goods and services.

Neoliberalism: an economic school of thought that advocates the shift of control over the economy from the public sector to the private sector to the ultimate benefit of all.

Nongovernmental organization: an organization that is neither a business nor affiliated with a government.

Now-developed country (NDC): a term used by Ha-Joon Chang to refer to countries that have already industrialized using non-neoliberal policies and institutions.

Policy: a rule determined by the decision of government leaders.

Political economy: the study of economics in relation to politics.

Political science: an academic discipline concerned with the study of governance, power relations, and the state.

Poverty: a condition in which individuals lack a minimum level of resources, determined as either a relative or an absolute measure, to achieve a necessary quality of life.

Property rights: socially or legally defined rules that protect the ownership of physical or intellectual property.

Protectionism: an economic policy in which taxes or regulations are imposed by a government to penalize trade between countries in order to protect a nation's industry or industrial profits.

Recession: a period of slowdown in economic activity and decrease in a country's wealth.

Reverse engineer: to deconstruct an object or a concept into its constituent parts for the purpose of understanding how it works and replicating its design.

Savings rate: the amount of money citizens deduct from their income and set aside for the future.

Social welfare: financial or other protections for a society's most vulnerable citizens or for those in specific kinds of need.

Sociology: an academic discipline concerned with the social behavior of individuals, groups, and societies.

State subsidies: assistance in the form of cash, investments, or other benefits awarded to groups, individuals, or businesses by the state in order to alleviate challenges to their success.

Structural adjustment programs: a system employed by the World Bank and the International Monetary Fund in which loans are given to countries experiencing economic crises on condition that the countries institute a series of economic reforms.

Tariff: a tax imposed on a country's imports or exports.

Third World: a general term that refers loosely to the least economically developed and least industrialized nations of the world.

Trade balance: the difference between the monetary value of a country's exports and its imports.

United Nations: an international organization, established in 1945, intended to encourage cooperation between states and the peaceful settlement of political and economic conflicts.

United Nations Development Program: a branch of the United Nations, established in 1965, devoted to promoting economic and social development among member states through advocacy and aid programs.

Urbanization: a process in which a population shifts from rural to urban areas and experiences social transformation as a result.

Washington Consensus: a set of 10 neoliberal economic policies recommended to developing countries by international financial institutions as a standard means for reform to encourage economic growth.

World Bank: an international organization, established in 1944, that provides loans to developing countries primarily for investment in infrastructure and industrialization.

World Trade Organization: an international organization, established in 1995, that is responsible for establishing the rules of trade between nations as well as mediating and adjudicating on international trade disputes.

World War II: a global conflict that lasted from 1939 to 1945 and which subsequently led to its most obvious victors, the United States and the Soviet Union, confronting each other in an ideologically driven conflict, the Cold War, which saw democracy and capitalism pitted against an authoritarian form of communism.

PEOPLE MENTIONED IN THE TEXT

Paul Bairoch (1930–99) was an economic historian who specialized in global economic history.

Seb Bytyci is a researcher at the University of York who specializes in public policy.

Park Chung-Hee (1917–79) was a South Korean general and dictator. He was known for leading South Korea through a period of rapid economic growth and transformation, albeit at the cost of its citizens' political and democratic rights.

Rafael Correa (b. 1963) was elected president of the Republic of Ecuador in 2007. An economist by profession, he is the leader of the democratic socialist PAIS Alliance.

William Easterly (b. 1957) is an American development economist. He is known for his criticism of international development aid, and his view that the world's poor should be empowered to create their own solutions to development problems.

Alexander Hamilton (1757–1804) was one of the founding fathers of the United States of America, and the first secretary of the United States Treasury. He was a staunch advocate of protectionist economic policies to support the development of early American industry.

Douglas Irwin (b. 1962) is an American economist. He is known for his research and publications on the history of international trade.

John Maynard Keynes (1883–1946) was an English economist. He was the founder of Keynesian economics, and developed the theory that macroeconomic economic cycles (economic cycles at the level of the state) could be managed by regulating the levels of supply and demand in an economy.

Shahrukh Rafi Khan is a development economist and visiting professor of economics at Mount Holyoke College.

Charles Kindleberger (1910–2003) was an American economic historian. He specialized in economic and financial crises, and became well known for his work on the relationship between economic and political power.

Anne Kreuger (b. 1934) is an American economist and served as chief economist of the World Bank from 1982 to 1986.

Simon Kuznets (1901–85) was an American economist, economic historian, and Nobel Prize winner. He is best known for the "Kuznets Curve," which depicts the relationship between income inequality and economic growth.

William Arthur Lewis (1915–91) was a Saint Lucian development economist. He developed the "Lewis Model," which explains economic development as the result of a transition of labor resources from subsistence to capitalism.

Justin Yifu Lin (b. 1952) is a Chinese development economist. He was chief economist at the World Bank from 2008 to 2012.

Friedrich List (1789–1846) was a German American economist. He pioneered the study of economic history as a means for evaluating economic policy.

Karl Marx (1818–83) was a German political philosopher and economist. The founder of Marxist thought, he argued that human societies progress through class struggle.

Peter Nolan is a professor of management at the University of Cambridge. He specializes in globalization and corporate governance in East Asian economies.

Gabriel Palma (b. 1947) is a Chilean economist at the University of Cambridge. He specializes in alternative approaches to economic theory and history.

Karl Polanyi (1886–1964) was a Hungarian American economic historian. He was a prominent opponent of traditional economic history narratives and argued that markets were created and engineered by the state.

James Putzel is a professor of development studies at the London School of Economics. He specializes in agrarian reform and development in fragile or crisis states.

Ronald Reagan (1911–2004) was president of the United States from 1981 to 1989.

Erik Reinert (b. 1949) is a Norwegian development economist specializing in economic history. He is an outspoken critic of free trade as a tool for economic development in developing countries.

Paul Rosenstein-Rodan (1902–85) was a Polish economist. He argued that only large-scale, "big push" investments could create economic development in developing countries.

Walt Rostow (1916–2003) was an American economist and political scientist. He was best known for his strong support of free markets and for his book outlining a theory on the stages of economic growth.

Robert Rowthorn (b. 1939) is a British economist. He is known for his Marxist views and his criticism of capitalism.

Ajit Singh (1940–2015) was an Indian economist. He was best known for his research on businesses and industrialization in developing countries.

Adam Smith (1723–90) was a Scottish philosopher and political economist. He is considered the father of the discipline of economics, having authored its first major work.

Joseph Stiglitz (b. 1943) is an American economist and Nobel Prize winner, and was chief economist of the World Bank from 1997 to 2000. He is known for his criticism of neoliberal development policies following his departure from the World Bank.

Margaret Thatcher (1925–2013) was prime minister of the United Kingdom from 1979 to 1990.

John Toye (b. 1942) is a British development economist at the University of Oxford and the School of Oriental and African Studies, University of London. He specializes in international economic institutions and the history of economic thought.

Martin Wolf (b. 1946) is a British journalist, chief economics commentator at the *Financial Times*, and considered one of the world's most prominent writers on economics.

WORKS CITED

WORKS CITED

Bairoch, Paul. *Economics and World History: Myths and Paradoxes*. Chicago, IL: University of Chicago Press, 1993.

Bytyci, Seb. "Review—Kicking Away the Ladder: Development Strategy in Historical Perspective," *ID: International Dialogue, a Multidisciplinary Journal of World Affairs* 3 (2013): 183–6.

Chang, Ha-Joon. *23 Things They Don't Tell You About Capitalism*. New York: Bloomsbury Press, 2010.

_____. *Bad Samaritans: The Myth of Free Trade and the Secret History of Capitalism*. New York: Bloomsbury Press, 2008.

_____. "Economic History of the Developed World: Lessons for Africa." Lecture, Eminent Speakers Program of the African Development Bank, February 26, 2009.

_____. "Economists Who Have Influenced Me." Accessed January 12, 2016. http://hajoonchang.net/economists-who-have-influenced-me/.

_____. *Kicking Away the Ladder: Development Strategy in Historical Perspective*. London: Anthem Press, 2003.

_____. "Kicking Away the Ladder: How the Economic and Intellectual Histories of Capitalism Have Been Re-written to Justify Neo-liberal Capitalism." *Post-Autistic Economics Review* 15, article 3 (2002). http://www.paecon.net/PAEtexts/Chang1.htm.

_____. "The Political Economy of Industrial Policy in Korea." *Cambridge Journal of Economics* 17 (1993): 131–57.

_____. "Response to Martin Wolf's 'The Growth of Nations'." *Financial Times*, August 3, 2007. Accessed January 12, 2016. http://www.cepr.net/documents/publications/FT_HaJoon.pdf.

Chang, Kyung-Sup, Ben Fine, and Linda Weiss, eds. *Developmental Politics in Transition: The Neoliberal Era and Beyond*. London: Palgrave Macmillan, 2012.

Correa, Rafael. "Presentación del libro 'El rostro oculto del TLC.'" *La Insignia*, May 20, 2006.

Democracy Now. "Economist Ha-Joon Chang on 'The Myth of Free Trade and the Secret History of Capitalism.'" *Democracy Now*, March 10, 2009. Accessed November 10, 2015. http://www.democracynow.org/2009/3/10/economist_ha_joon_chang_on_the.

Easterly, William. "The Anarchy of Success." *New York Review of Books* 56, no. 15 (2009): 28–30.

Goodwin, Neva R. "Leontief Prize 2005: Ha-Joon Chang." Speech, 2005 Leontief Prize Award Presentation, October 27, 2005.

Hodgson, Geoffrey and Shuxia Jiang. "The Economics of Corruption and the Corruption of Economics." *Journal of Economic Issues* 41, no. 4 (2007): 1043–61.

Irwin, Douglas. "Book Review of Kicking Away the Ladder by Ha-Joon Chang." *EH.NET*, April 2004. Accessed January 12, 2016. http://eh.net/book_reviews/ kicking-away-the-ladder-development-strategy-in-historical-perspective.

Khan, Shahrukh Rafi. *A History of Development Economics Thought: Challenges and Counter-challenges*. New York: Routledge, 2014.

Kuznets, Simon. *Toward a Theory of Economic Growth: With Reflections on the Economic Growth of Modern Nations*. London: Norton, 1968.

Lewis, W. Arthur. *The Theory of Economic Growth*. Chicago, IL: R. D. Irwin, 1955.

Lin, Justin Yifu. *The Quest for Prosperity: How Developing Economies Can Take Off*. Princeton, NJ: Princeton University Press, 2012.

Monbiot, George. "If You Think We're Done with Neoliberalism, Think Again." *Guardian*, January 14, 2013.

Peet, Richard, and Elaine Hartwick. *Theories of Development: Contentions, Arguments, Alternatives* (3rd Ed.). New York: Guilford Press, 2015.

Prospect. "World Thinkers 2014: The Results." *Prospect*, May 2014. Accessed January 12, 2016. http://www.prospectmagazine.co.uk/features/world-thinkers-2014-the-results.

Reinert, Erik S. *How Rich Countries Got Rich ... and Why Poor Countries Stay Poor*. London: Constable, 2007.

Rostow, Walt. *The Stages of Economic Growth*. Cambridge: Cambridge University Press, 1960.

Smith, Adam. *An Inquiry into the Nature and Causes of the Wealth of Nations*. London: W. Strahan & T. Cadell, 1776.

Stiglitz, Joseph E. "Intellectual Property Rights, the Pool of Knowledge, and Innovation." NBER Working Paper 20014 (March 2014).

Toye, John. "Changing Perspectives in Development Economics." In *Rethinking Development Economics*, edited by Ha-Joon Chang, 21–40. London and New York: Anthem Press, 2003.

Von Werlhof, Claudia. "Neoliberal Globalization: Is There an Alternative to Plundering the Earth?" In *The Global Economic Crisis: The Great Depression of the XXI Century*, edited by Michel Chossudovsky and Andrew Gavin Marshall, 116–45. Montreal: Global Research Publishers, 2010.

THE MACAT LIBRARY
BY DISCIPLINE

AFRICANA STUDIES

Chinua Achebe's *An Image of Africa: Racism in Conrad's Heart of Darkness*
W. E. B. Du Bois's *The Souls of Black Folk*
Zora Neale Huston's *Characteristics of Negro Expression*
Martin Luther King Jr's *Why We Can't Wait*
Toni Morrison's *Playing in the Dark: Whiteness in the American Literary Imagination*

ANTHROPOLOGY

Arjun Appadurai's *Modernity at Large: Cultural Dimensions of Globalisation*
Philippe Ariès's *Centuries of Childhood*
Franz Boas's *Race, Language and Culture*
Kim Chan & Renée Mauborgne's *Blue Ocean Strategy*
Jared Diamond's *Guns, Germs & Steel: the Fate of Human Societies*
Jared Diamond's *Collapse: How Societies Choose to Fail or Survive*
E. E. Evans-Pritchard's *Witchcraft, Oracles and Magic Among the Azande*
James Ferguson's *The Anti-Politics Machine*
Clifford Geertz's *The Interpretation of Cultures*
David Graeber's *Debt: the First 5000 Years*
Karen Ho's *Liquidated: An Ethnography of Wall Street*
Geert Hofstede's *Culture's Consequences: Comparing Values, Behaviors, Institutes and Organizations across Nations*
Claude Lévi-Strauss's *Structural Anthropology*
Jay Macleod's *Ain't No Makin' It: Aspirations and Attainment in a Low-Income Neighborhood*
Saba Mahmood's *The Politics of Piety: The Islamic Revival and the Feminist Subject*
Marcel Mauss's *The Gift*

BUSINESS

Jean Lave & Etienne Wenger's *Situated Learning*
Theodore Levitt's *Marketing Myopia*
Burton G. Malkiel's *A Random Walk Down Wall Street*
Douglas McGregor's *The Human Side of Enterprise*
Michael Porter's *Competitive Strategy: Creating and Sustaining Superior Performance*
John Kotter's *Leading Change*
C. K. Prahalad & Gary Hamel's *The Core Competence of the Corporation*

CRIMINOLOGY

Michelle Alexander's *The New Jim Crow: Mass Incarceration in the Age of Colorblindness*
Michael R. Gottfredson & Travis Hirschi's *A General Theory of Crime*
Richard Herrnstein & Charles A. Murray's *The Bell Curve: Intelligence and Class Structure in American Life*
Elizabeth Loftus's *Eyewitness Testimony*
Jay Macleod's *Ain't No Makin' It: Aspirations and Attainment in a Low-Income Neighborhood*
Philip Zimbardo's *The Lucifer Effect*

ECONOMICS

Janet Abu-Lughod's *Before European Hegemony*
Ha-Joon Chang's *Kicking Away the Ladder*
David Brion Davis's *The Problem of Slavery in the Age of Revolution*
Milton Friedman's *The Role of Monetary Policy*
Milton Friedman's *Capitalism and Freedom*
David Graeber's *Debt: the First 5000 Years*
Friedrich Hayek's *The Road to Serfdom*
Karen Ho's *Liquidated: An Ethnography of Wall Street*

John Maynard Keynes's *The General Theory of Employment, Interest and Money*
Charles P. Kindleberger's *Manias, Panics and Crashes*
Robert Lucas's *Why Doesn't Capital Flow from Rich to Poor Countries?*
Burton G. Malkiel's *A Random Walk Down Wall Street*
Thomas Robert Malthus's *An Essay on the Principle of Population*
Karl Marx's *Capital*
Thomas Piketty's *Capital in the Twenty-First Century*
Amartya Sen's *Development as Freedom*
Adam Smith's *The Wealth of Nations*
Nassim Nicholas Taleb's *The Black Swan: The Impact of the Highly Improbable*
Amos Tversky's & Daniel Kahneman's *Judgment under Uncertainty: Heuristics and Biases*
Mahbub Ul Haq's *Reflections on Human Development*
Max Weber's *The Protestant Ethic and the Spirit of Capitalism*

FEMINISM AND GENDER STUDIES

Judith Butler's *Gender Trouble*
Simone De Beauvoir's *The Second Sex*
Michel Foucault's *History of Sexuality*
Betty Friedan's *The Feminine Mystique*
Saba Mahmood's *The Politics of Piety: The Islamic Revival and the Feminist Subject*
Joan Wallach Scott's *Gender and the Politics of History*
Mary Wollstonecraft's *A Vindication of the Rights of Woman*
Virginia Woolf's *A Room of One's Own*

GEOGRAPHY

The Brundtland Report's *Our Common Future*
Rachel Carson's *Silent Spring*
Charles Darwin's *On the Origin of Species*
James Ferguson's *The Anti-Politics Machine*
Jane Jacobs's *The Death and Life of Great American Cities*
James Lovelock's *Gaia: A New Look at Life on Earth*
Amartya Sen's *Development as Freedom*
Mathis Wackernagel & William Rees's *Our Ecological Footprint*

HISTORY

Janet Abu-Lughod's *Before European Hegemony*
Benedict Anderson's *Imagined Communities*
Bernard Bailyn's *The Ideological Origins of the American Revolution*
Hanna Batatu's *The Old Social Classes And The Revolutionary Movements Of Iraq*
Christopher Browning's *Ordinary Men: Reserve Police Batallion 101 and the Final Solution in Poland*
Edmund Burke's *Reflections on the Revolution in France*
William Cronon's *Nature's Metropolis: Chicago And The Great West*
Alfred W. Crosby's *The Columbian Exchange*
Hamid Dabashi's *Iran: A People Interrupted*
David Brion Davis's *The Problem of Slavery in the Age of Revolution*
Nathalie Zemon Davis's *The Return of Martin Guerre*
Jared Diamond's *Guns, Germs & Steel: the Fate of Human Societies*
Frank Dikotter's *Mao's Great Famine*
John W Dower's *War Without Mercy: Race And Power In The Pacific War*
W. E. B. Du Bois's *The Souls of Black Folk*
Richard J. Evans's *In Defence of History*
Lucien Febvre's *The Problem of Unbelief in the 16th Century*
Sheila Fitzpatrick's *Everyday Stalinism*

The Macat Library By Discipline

Eric Foner's *Reconstruction: America's Unfinished Revolution, 1863-1877*
Michel Foucault's *Discipline and Punish*
Michel Foucault's *History of Sexuality*
Francis Fukuyama's *The End of History and the Last Man*
John Lewis Gaddis's *We Now Know: Rethinking Cold War History*
Ernest Gellner's *Nations and Nationalism*
Eugene Genovese's *Roll, Jordan, Roll: The World the Slaves Made*
Carlo Ginzburg's *The Night Battles*
Daniel Goldhagen's *Hitler's Willing Executioners*
Jack Goldstone's *Revolution and Rebellion in the Early Modern World*
Antonio Gramsci's *The Prison Notebooks*
Alexander Hamilton, John Jay & James Madison's *The Federalist Papers*
Christopher Hill's *The World Turned Upside Down*
Carole Hillenbrand's *The Crusades: Islamic Perspectives*
Thomas Hobbes's *Leviathan*
Eric Hobsbawm's *The Age Of Revolution*
John A. Hobson's *Imperialism: A Study*
Albert Hourani's *History of the Arab Peoples*
Samuel P. Huntington's *The Clash of Civilizations and the Remaking of World Order*
C. L. R. James's *The Black Jacobins*
Tony Judt's *Postwar: A History of Europe Since 1945*
Ernst Kantorowicz's *The King's Two Bodies: A Study in Medieval Political Theology*
Paul Kennedy's *The Rise and Fall of the Great Powers*
Ian Kershaw's *The "Hitler Myth": Image and Reality in the Third Reich*
John Maynard Keynes's *The General Theory of Employment, Interest and Money*
Charles P. Kindleberger's *Manias, Panics and Crashes*
Martin Luther King Jr's *Why We Can't Wait*
Henry Kissinger's *World Order: Reflections on the Character of Nations and the Course of History*
Thomas Kuhn's *The Structure of Scientific Revolutions*
Georges Lefebvre's *The Coming of the French Revolution*
John Locke's *Two Treatises of Government*
Niccolò Machiavelli's *The Prince*
Thomas Robert Malthus's *An Essay on the Principle of Population*
Mahmood Mamdani's *Citizen and Subject: Contemporary Africa And The Legacy Of Late Colonialism*
Karl Marx's *Capital*
Stanley Milgram's *Obedience to Authority*
John Stuart Mill's *On Liberty*
Thomas Paine's *Common Sense*
Thomas Paine's *Rights of Man*
Geoffrey Parker's *Global Crisis: War, Climate Change and Catastrophe in the Seventeenth Century*
Jonathan Riley-Smith's *The First Crusade and the Idea of Crusading*
Jean-Jacques Rousseau's *The Social Contract*
Joan Wallach Scott's *Gender and the Politics of History*
Theda Skocpol's *States and Social Revolutions*
Adam Smith's *The Wealth of Nations*
Timothy Snyder's *Bloodlands: Europe Between Hitler and Stalin*
Sun Tzu's *The Art of War*
Keith Thomas's *Religion and the Decline of Magic*
Thucydides's *The History of the Peloponnesian War*
Frederick Jackson Turner's *The Significance of the Frontier in American History*
Odd Arne Westad's *The Global Cold War: Third World Interventions And The Making Of Our Times*

LITERATURE

Chinua Achebe's *An Image of Africa: Racism in Conrad's Heart of Darkness*
Roland Barthes's *Mythologies*
Homi K. Bhabha's *The Location of Culture*
Judith Butler's *Gender Trouble*
Simone De Beauvoir's *The Second Sex*
Ferdinand De Saussure's *Course in General Linguistics*
T. S. Eliot's *The Sacred Wood: Essays on Poetry and Criticism*
Zora Neale Huston's *Characteristics of Negro Expression*
Toni Morrison's *Playing in the Dark: Whiteness in the American Literary Imagination*
Edward Said's *Orientalism*
Gayatri Chakravorty Spivak's *Can the Subaltern Speak?*
Mary Wollstonecraft's *A Vindication of the Rights of Women*
Virginia Woolf's *A Room of One's Own*

PHILOSOPHY

Elizabeth Anscombe's *Modern Moral Philosophy*
Hannah Arendt's *The Human Condition*
Aristotle's *Metaphysics*
Aristotle's *Nicomachean Ethics*
Edmund Gettier's *Is Justified True Belief Knowledge?*
Georg Wilhelm Friedrich Hegel's *Phenomenology of Spirit*
David Hume's *Dialogues Concerning Natural Religion*
David Hume's *The Enquiry for Human Understanding*
Immanuel Kant's *Religion within the Boundaries of Mere Reason*
Immanuel Kant's *Critique of Pure Reason*
Søren Kierkegaard's *The Sickness Unto Death*
Søren Kierkegaard's *Fear and Trembling*
C. S. Lewis's *The Abolition of Man*
Alasdair MacIntyre's *After Virtue*
Marcus Aurelius's *Meditations*
Friedrich Nietzsche's *On the Genealogy of Morality*
Friedrich Nietzsche's *Beyond Good and Evil*
Plato's *Republic*
Plato's *Symposium*
Jean-Jacques Rousseau's *The Social Contract*
Gilbert Ryle's *The Concept of Mind*
Baruch Spinoza's *Ethics*
Sun Tzu's *The Art of War*
Ludwig Wittgenstein's *Philosophical Investigations*

POLITICS

Benedict Anderson's *Imagined Communities*
Aristotle's *Politics*
Bernard Bailyn's *The Ideological Origins of the American Revolution*
Edmund Burke's *Reflections on the Revolution in France*
John C. Calhoun's *A Disquisition on Government*
Ha-Joon Chang's *Kicking Away the Ladder*
Hamid Dabashi's *Iran: A People Interrupted*
Hamid Dabashi's *Theology of Discontent: The Ideological Foundation of the Islamic Revolution in Iran*
Robert Dahl's *Democracy and its Critics*
Robert Dahl's *Who Governs?*
David Brion Davis's *The Problem of Slavery in the Age of Revolution*

The Macat Library By Discipline

Alexis De Tocqueville's *Democracy in America*
James Ferguson's *The Anti-Politics Machine*
Frank Dikotter's *Mao's Great Famine*
Sheila Fitzpatrick's *Everyday Stalinism*
Eric Foner's *Reconstruction: America's Unfinished Revolution, 1863-1877*
Milton Friedman's *Capitalism and Freedom*
Francis Fukuyama's *The End of History and the Last Man*
John Lewis Gaddis's *We Now Know: Rethinking Cold War History*
Ernest Gellner's *Nations and Nationalism*
David Graeber's *Debt: the First 5000 Years*
Antonio Gramsci's *The Prison Notebooks*
Alexander Hamilton, John Jay & James Madison's *The Federalist Papers*
Friedrich Hayek's *The Road to Serfdom*
Christopher Hill's *The World Turned Upside Down*
Thomas Hobbes's *Leviathan*
John A. Hobson's *Imperialism: A Study*
Samuel P. Huntington's *The Clash of Civilizations and the Remaking of World Order*
Tony Judt's *Postwar: A History of Europe Since 1945*
David C. Kang's *China Rising: Peace, Power and Order in East Asia*
Paul Kennedy's *The Rise and Fall of Great Powers*
Robert Keohane's *After Hegemony*
Martin Luther King Jr.'s *Why We Can't Wait*
Henry Kissinger's *World Order: Reflections on the Character of Nations and the Course of History*
John Locke's *Two Treatises of Government*
Niccolò Machiavelli's *The Prince*
Thomas Robert Malthus's *An Essay on the Principle of Population*
Mahmood Mamdani's *Citizen and Subject: Contemporary Africa And The Legacy Of Late Colonialism*
Karl Marx's *Capital*
John Stuart Mill's *On Liberty*
John Stuart Mill's *Utilitarianism*
Hans Morgenthau's *Politics Among Nations*
Thomas Paine's *Common Sense*
Thomas Paine's *Rights of Man*
Thomas Piketty's *Capital in the Twenty-First Century*
Robert D. Putman's *Bowling Alone*
John Rawls's *Theory of Justice*
Jean-Jacques Rousseau's *The Social Contract*
Theda Skocpol's *States and Social Revolutions*
Adam Smith's *The Wealth of Nations*
Sun Tzu's *The Art of War*
Henry David Thoreau's *Civil Disobedience*
Thucydides's *The History of the Peloponnesian War*
Kenneth Waltz's *Theory of International Politics*
Max Weber's *Politics as a Vocation*
Odd Arne Westad's *The Global Cold War: Third World Interventions And The Making Of Our Times*

POSTCOLONIAL STUDIES

Roland Barthes's *Mythologies*
Frantz Fanon's *Black Skin, White Masks*
Homi K. Bhabha's *The Location of Culture*
Gustavo Gutiérrez's *A Theology of Liberation*
Edward Said's *Orientalism*
Gayatri Chakravorty Spivak's *Can the Subaltern Speak?*

PSYCHOLOGY

Gordon Allport's *The Nature of Prejudice*
Alan Baddeley & Graham Hitch's *Aggression: A Social Learning Analysis*
Albert Bandura's *Aggression: A Social Learning Analysis*
Leon Festinger's *A Theory of Cognitive Dissonance*
Sigmund Freud's *The Interpretation of Dreams*
Betty Friedan's *The Feminine Mystique*
Michael R. Gottfredson & Travis Hirschi's *A General Theory of Crime*
Eric Hoffer's *The True Believer: Thoughts on the Nature of Mass Movements*
William James's *Principles of Psychology*
Elizabeth Loftus's *Eyewitness Testimony*
A. H. Maslow's *A Theory of Human Motivation*
Stanley Milgram's *Obedience to Authority*
Steven Pinker's *The Better Angels of Our Nature*
Oliver Sacks's *The Man Who Mistook His Wife For a Hat*
Richard Thaler & Cass Sunstein's *Nudge: Improving Decisions About Health, Wealth and Happiness*
Amos Tversky's *Judgment under Uncertainty: Heuristics and Biases*
Philip Zimbardo's *The Lucifer Effect*

SCIENCE

Rachel Carson's *Silent Spring*
William Cronon's *Nature's Metropolis: Chicago And The Great West*
Alfred W. Crosby's *The Columbian Exchange*
Charles Darwin's *On the Origin of Species*
Richard Dawkin's *The Selfish Gene*
Thomas Kuhn's *The Structure of Scientific Revolutions*
Geoffrey Parker's *Global Crisis: War, Climate Change and Catastrophe in the Seventeenth Century*
Mathis Wackernagel & William Rees's *Our Ecological Footprint*

SOCIOLOGY

Michelle Alexander's *The New Jim Crow: Mass Incarceration in the Age of Colorblindness*
Gordon Allport's *The Nature of Prejudice*
Albert Bandura's *Aggression: A Social Learning Analysis*
Hanna Batatu's *The Old Social Classes And The Revolutionary Movements Of Iraq*
Ha-Joon Chang's *Kicking Away the Ladder*
W. E. B. Du Bois's *The Souls of Black Folk*
Émile Durkheim's *On Suicide*
Frantz Fanon's *Black Skin, White Masks*
Frantz Fanon's *The Wretched of the Earth*
Eric Foner's *Reconstruction: America's Unfinished Revolution, 1863-1877*
Eugene Genovese's *Roll, Jordan, Roll: The World the Slaves Made*
Jack Goldstone's *Revolution and Rebellion in the Early Modern World*
Antonio Gramsci's *The Prison Notebooks*
Richard Herrnstein & Charles A Murray's *The Bell Curve: Intelligence and Class Structure in American Life*
Eric Hoffer's *The True Believer: Thoughts on the Nature of Mass Movements*
Jane Jacobs's *The Death and Life of Great American Cities*
Robert Lucas's *Why Doesn't Capital Flow from Rich to Poor Countries?*
Jay Macleod's *Ain't No Makin' It: Aspirations and Attainment in a Low Income Neighborhood*
Elaine May's *Homeward Bound: American Families in the Cold War Era*
Douglas McGregor's *The Human Side of Enterprise*
C. Wright Mills's *The Sociological Imagination*

The Macat Library By Discipline

Thomas Piketty's *Capital in the Twenty-First Century*
Robert D. Putman's *Bowling Alone*
David Riesman's *The Lonely Crowd: A Study of the Changing American Character*
Edward Said's *Orientalism*
Joan Wallach Scott's *Gender and the Politics of History*
Theda Skocpol's *States and Social Revolutions*
Max Weber's *The Protestant Ethic and the Spirit of Capitalism*

THEOLOGY

Augustine's *Confessions*
Benedict's *Rule of St Benedict*
Gustavo Gutiérrez's *A Theology of Liberation*
Carole Hillenbrand's *The Crusades: Islamic Perspectives*
David Hume's *Dialogues Concerning Natural Religion*
Immanuel Kant's *Religion within the Boundaries of Mere Reason*
Ernst Kantorowicz's *The King's Two Bodies: A Study in Medieval Political Theology*
Søren Kierkegaard's *The Sickness Unto Death*
C. S. Lewis's *The Abolition of Man*
Saba Mahmood's *The Politics of Piety: The Islamic Revival and the Feminist Subject*
Baruch Spinoza's *Ethics*
Keith Thomas's *Religion and the Decline of Magic*

COMING SOON

Chris Argyris's *The Individual and the Organisation*
Seyla Benhabib's *The Rights of Others*
Walter Benjamin's *The Work Of Art in the Age of Mechanical Reproduction*
John Berger's *Ways of Seeing*
Pierre Bourdieu's *Outline of a Theory of Practice*
Mary Douglas's *Purity and Danger*
Roland Dworkin's *Taking Rights Seriously*
James G. March's *Exploration and Exploitation in Organisational Learning*
Ikujiro Nonaka's *A Dynamic Theory of Organizational Knowledge Creation*
Griselda Pollock's *Vision and Difference*
Amartya Sen's *Inequality Re-Examined*
Susan Sontag's *On Photography*
Yasser Tabbaa's *The Transformation of Islamic Art*
Ludwig von Mises's *Theory of Money and Credit*

Macat Pairs

Analyse historical and modern issues from opposite sides of an argument. Pairs include:

RACE AND IDENTITY

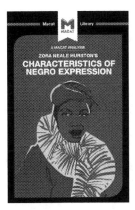

Zora Neale Hurston's
Characteristics of Negro Expression

Using material collected on anthropological expeditions to the South, Zora Neale Hurston explains how expression in African American culture in the early twentieth century departs from the art of white America. At the time, African American art was often criticized for copying white culture. For Hurston, this criticism misunderstood how art works. European tradition views art as something fixed. But Hurston describes a creative process that is alive, ever-changing, and largely improvisational. She maintains that African American art works through a process called 'mimicry'—where an imitated object or verbal pattern, for example, is reshaped and altered until it becomes something new, novel—and worthy of attention.

Frantz Fanon's
Black Skin, White Masks

Black Skin, White Masks offers a radical analysis of the psychological effects of colonization on the colonized.

Fanon witnessed the effects of colonization first hand both in his birthplace, Martinique, and again later in life when he worked as a psychiatrist in another French colony, Algeria. His text is uncompromising in form and argument. He dissects the dehumanizing effects of colonialism, arguing that it destroys the native sense of identity, forcing people to adapt to an alien set of values—including a core belief that they are inferior. This results in deep psychological trauma.

Fanon's work played a pivotal role in the civil rights movements of the 1960s.

Macat analyses are available from all good bookshops and libraries.

Access hundreds of analyses through one, multimedia tool.
Join free for one month **library.macat.com**

Macat Pairs

Analyse historical and modern issues from opposite sides of an argument. Pairs include:

INTERNATIONAL RELATIONS IN THE 21ST CENTURY

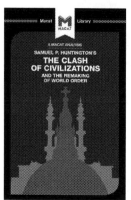

Samuel P. Huntington's
The Clash of Civilisations

In his highly influential 1996 book, Huntington offers a vision of a post-Cold War world in which conflict takes place not between competing ideologies but between cultures. The worst clash, he argues, will be between the Islamic world and the West: the West's arrogance and belief that its culture is a "gift" to the world will come into conflict with Islam's obstinacy and concern that its culture is under attack from a morally decadent "other."

Clash inspired much debate between different political schools of thought. But its greatest impact came in helping define American foreign policy in the wake of the 2001 terrorist attacks in New York and Washington.

Francis Fukuyama's
The End of History and the Last Man

Published in 1992, *The End of History and the Last Man* argues that capitalist democracy is the final destination for all societies. Fukuyama believed democracy triumphed during the Cold War because it lacks the "fundamental contradictions" inherent in communism and satisfies our yearning for freedom and equality. Democracy therefore marks the endpoint in the evolution of ideology, and so the "end of history." There will still be "events," but no fundamental change in ideology.

Printed in the United States
by Baker & Taylor Publisher Services